IN THE MIDDLE OF THE NIGHT

Surviving the Pain of Profound Loss

IN THE MIDDLE OF THE NIGHT

Surviving the Pain of Profound Loss

BY

Dr. Ronnie Cheatwood

eBookstand

http://www.eBookstand.com
http://www.CyberRead.com

Published by
eBookstand
Division of CyberRead, Inc
1945_10

ISBN 1-58909-292-9

Printed in the United States of America

This Book is
In Loving Memory of
Brandon Michael Cheatwood
An adventurous young man
A trustworthy friend
A loving son
A compassionate brother

PREFACE

This book is the result of a very long and dark journey that continues today. In this journey I have written down thoughts, personal experiences, conversations, sermons, and entries in personal journals. From these notes came this book. Credit is given where credit is known. The reason I wrote this book is to make others more aware of God's presence in the darkest of times. He wants us to trust Him, so I trust He will use this to His glory.

I want to thank my beautiful wife and daughters for their encouragement. They were without me for many nights as I worked and prayed over this. They love me in spite of myself. As you read this book, my prayer is that God will give you what you need for today helping you to trust Him more in your own journey.

Found, forgiven, and forever His,
The Author

INTRODUCTION

When the doorbell rang at 3:00 AM on July 1, 2003, I knew. Opening the door and seeing several State Troopers, one of which held my son's drivers license in his hand, I knew. Hearing the officer ask me if a Brandon Cheatwood lived at this address and if I was his father, I knew. But still today, even though I have known for a while now, it is hard to believe my son walked out our door and never came back.

Brandon went on his first anniversary date with his girlfriend that Monday night. On the way home, he was in a crash involving a drunken driver. Brandon was pronounced dead at the scene at 11:50 PM June 30, 2003. The 17 year-old drunken driver was arrested and taken away without a scratch. Brandon could not be identified by his drivers license picture. The State Troopers led us to the morgue, and I had to identify him. Needless to say, it was a rough night.

I have seen very few things in my ministry that has more of an impact on an individual or a family than the death of someone they love. It brings reality into focus and no amount of prayer or pleading with God will change that reality. It is a confusing time as the pendulum of your emotions swings from anger to sadness. Living without this person seems impossible. You want this horrible situation to be over, but it lingers. It won't go away. It remains. When you think you are adjusting, it overwhelms you again. There are days when you simply have to tell yourself to get up one more time; just keep going one more day.

People attempt to help you, telling you they are there if you need them; just "a phone-call away." They are, but you are still alone. They tell you that God is with you, but all you can think of is where was He when my loved one died? He could have prevented this great loss but didn't. As some quote Romans 8:28 to you and say that all things happen for the good, you wonder if they would be quoting that verse if their loved one was in a grave. You really don't care what good might happen one day down the road. You are simply trying to survive today. It seems that everyone wants you to be fixed, to get back to "normal" again. But no amount of words or wishes will relieve you from this journey. You must travel this road, and you don't know how.

I am a pastor. I had preached and taught theology for many years. That night I locked myself in our bathroom and had to decide if I really believed what I had been preaching. Sliding down the wall, there was really only one thing I had to establish as true. Is Jesus alive? Is there a chance that my loved one will walk with me again some day? I knew that if Jesus was alive; everything else was relevant and I could survive this. In the days to come, I had to reestablish what I believed in light of what had happened. The result of that journey is this book.

God led me through one particular chapter of the Bible, John 21. He taught me what was going on in my life could be seen in the life of the Apostle Peter. Peter had experienced the loss of a loved one–Jesus. Jesus had been crucified and buried. Peter had failed miserably the night of his Savior's death by denying he knew Him. Peter's loss was tremendous, and his life was in the depths of despair. Peter knew Jesus had risen from the dead, but this too was something he would have to work through. Grief is something you have to work through. As Peter learned, you can work through this with the help of Jesus. Loss is a part of living. We will all lose people in our lives. The only thing we can do is find the way to deal with that loss.

King David wrote in Psalm 23 of walking through the valley of the shadow of death. I have read and listened to many who have said he wrote this when he was a young shepherd boy on a hill watching his sheep. I won't argue that point. Personally I believe he wrote this Psalm when he was old, and he was looking back. This valley he wrote of might have been the valley he walked when his son Absalom was killed. Listen to his words in 2 Samuel 18:33, "The king was stunned. Heartbroken, he went up to the room over the gate and wept. As he wept he cried out,

'O my son Absalom, my dear, dear son Absalom!

Why not me rather than you, my death and not yours,

O Absalom, my dear, dear son!'" (The Message)

I have walked this valley and it is slow and long. I have looked back where I have been wondering how it all happened. I have looked up from the abyss searching ahead for what is yet to be. I have found myself doubting many things. Many days have been spent wondering if perhaps my faith has been simply a routine, a crutch of comfort, or real at all. I have even wondered if what I believe is true and safe.

On the other hand, there have been times, moments of truth, unlike any before in my life. There have been times of God's presence, so real, I could feel His hand in mine. I have realized the presence of strength and courage in my life that I did not produce. I have come to know my God in ways I never have before. I have found that not only is He everything the Bible says He is, but more. Death is an undeniable reality. It is the most obvious scar of the fall of man. It is the ultimate symbol of separation and mortality. That is why there is an empty tomb. Jesus defeated this enemy over two thousand years ago, and He remains alive today. I am no pillar of unwavering faith, so I take a deep breath each day and believe that fact. He is alive and He will comfort me. He will carry me. He will come for me one day.

I hope this book will help you if you have lost a loved one. If you have never lost a loved one, perhaps this book can be a tool to help someone you know who has lost a loved one. There is life after loss; if you have help. This is one way God helped me. My hope is that it will help you also. Jesus Christ will help you find your way in the middle of the night. Trust Him, He is alive.

CHAPTER ONE

SOMETIMES FAILURE IS IN THE WILL OF GOD

Everyone wishes they could go back and change one day of their life. The day of the crash is the day I wish could be changed. I miss my son every day. Brandon was fun to be around, with a very dry sense of humor. He was very intelligent, with an almost photographic memory. He had taken college courses while in high school, graduating with an advanced academic diploma. His plans included becoming a medical doctor; using his skills on the mission field in a Spanish speaking country. Being a medical missionary had been his desire even when he was a small boy. He had taken a mission trip to Trinidad with Teen Missions when he was a teenager, coming back absolutely sure of his calling from God. He was an uncommon young man. His priorities were not material like most teenagers. He invested his time and energy in others. Young women he knew came to us after his death and told us how he was always a gentleman, going out of his way to make them feel safe. His friends told us of his ability to make any situation more enjoyable with his adventurous spirit and his dry wit. He was a loving son, a wonderful brother, and an incredible friend. He is missed by everyone that knew him. He had earned my trust and respect as a young man and as my son. Therefore, I did not want to look back and see that I had failed him in any way. But the question that kept running through my mind was, who had failed that night?

The sovereignty of God is both security and frustration for the child of God. There is security in the truth that God never loses control of any situation, but frustration in the truth that we never really have control of the outcome of the situation. After the crash, the investigation began and the events were laid out moment by moment leading up to Brandon's death. The State Troopers interviewed, photographed, examined, and formulated for several weeks. Every detail leading up to the crash was considered. After talking to them and the District Attorney, I playing the scenario in my mind over and over. I kept asking the same question to myself and to others, why didn't God change just one small event?

The Bible teaches the sovereignty of God, which means He is completely in control. Therefore, if God could have delayed Brandon for just a few minutes, given him a flat tire, sent a hailstorm, caused an earthquake, anything and the crash would have been diverted. I almost told Brandon to take our SUV, which was taller than his car, but didn't. Could my choice have changed the outcome? I kept asking myself if I had failed in some way to protect my son. And what of the drunken driver? Did his choice to drink and drive control the outcome of that night? Was the drunk driver ultimately to blame? Who had failed, and how could this failure have been diverted? How much control do we have? How much control does God have in these, and in every situation? Do we have the freedom to choose? If we do, can our choices or someone else's choice alter the will of God for that situation?

I have arrived at this answer. We have the freedom to choose, but only God determines the outcome of the choice. We must have the freedom to choose, or we cannot have faith or love. Faith is a choice, and so is love. Faith is the choice to believe. Love is the choice to accept. Both faith and love are our side of the equation. Sovereignty is God's side. He controls the outcome of our choices. As far as God's will is concerned there was no failure that day. There was a plan that we were unaware of. God executed that plan with intricate precision and with eternal results.

In the Scripture before us, the plan of God is revealed in the very first verse. "After these things Jesus shewed himself again to the disciples at the sea of Tiberias; and on this wise shewed he himself" (John 21:1 KJV). Note that Jesus "shewed Himself" is mentioned not just once, but twice in this single verse. Maybe God is trying to make a point here. The point is Jesus wants us to know Him. As these men chose to go fishing, God was going to make sure the result of their choice was to see Jesus in a way they had never seen Him before. This verse also contains another important fact concerning our choices. It says, "After these things..." In the preceding chapters of the book of John, Jesus has been crucified, died, and buried in a graveyard. Every one of the apostles had abandoned Jesus when He was arrested. Peter denied knowing Jesus not once but three times. He felt he was a failure. They all felt they were failures. Their plans had failed but God's plan had not failed even in a graveyard.

Death is challenging to anyone's faith, even to those who had walked, talked, eaten, and laughed with Christ. These men were grieving. Their emotions are reacting to uncontrollable choices made by others. It is here they are coming to terms with the truth of God's sovereignty. In the past three years they had seen the dead raised. Now the one that raised the dead was dead Himself. Death and the collateral damage that ensued was not how they thought their choices would have played out. They each had chosen, others had chosen, and then Jesus chose and died. God's sovereignty meant that the result of these choices would be our ability to know Him.

Jesus wants you to know Him. He wants you to know He is enough, and you can trust Him. You may be afraid of the entire concept of death. You may have stood at the tomb of a loved one and wept. You may get a phone call, hear a doorbell, or listen across a physician's desk and hear your plans fade into the darkness. Every week I stand in a graveyard where the tombstones of my son, my brother, and my father remind me of the men I have known and now miss. Every week I walk away from that graveyard to begin another week without them. I often pause to consider the reasons to keep going. The Bible teaches that it is not a 'what' that keeps you going, but a 'Who' that keeps you going .

Jesus is the reason you can go on. Jesus conquered death and the grave. Those who trust Him have what He has, the way out of the grave. To be honest, I really didn't feel happy that my loss was helping the population growth of heaven. Although I did find comfort in the promise that my son was not lost forever. Brandon was safe and waiting for me to join him.

Psalm 116:15 says, "Precious in the sight of the Lord is the death of His saints." Why? Because they go to be with the Lord forever. If you do not know Jesus personally, now is the time to seek Him. He wants to be your Savior and your Lord and He wants you to live with Him forever. He wants all He has to be yours, that's why He came. He wants to know you right now, just as you are. Admit to Him your need and accept His gift of eternal life.

Does this mean nothing bad will ever happen again? No. As you know, bad things happen to everyone as well as good things. To accept Jesus Christ as your Savior does not mean the consequences of the sin in this world will suddenly vanish away for you. It does mean that your sins will be forgiven, and God will accept you into His Heaven when you leave this sinful world. We all have the choice to go through the difficulties of life either with or without a relationship with God. Without a relationship with God, there is no need to pray and no hope beyond the grave. But with a relationship with God, with Jesus Christ as your personal Savior, all that He has promised is yours. You have hope not only in this life but also in the life beyond the grave. If you do not know Jesus personally as your Savior all you have to do is ask Him. He will forgive you and accept you right now. He is alive, trust Him.

CHAPTER TWO

GOD IS BIGGER THAN I THOUGHT
YET CLOSER THAN I EVER IMAGINED

David Livingstone, the Nineteenth Century missionary from Scotland to Africa once wrote his statement of commitment. In these words you may see the cost of following Christ. He wrote, "Lord, send me anywhere, only go with me. Lay any burden on me, only sustain me. Sever any tie but the tie that binds me to Thyself." Anything you can hold in your hand you can lose, so hold what is precious to you in your heart. God says in Isaiah 55:8-9 (The Message) "I don't think the way you think. The way you work isn't the way I work. God's Decree. For as the sky soars high above earth, so the way I work surpasses the way you work, and the way I think is beyond the way you think." These verses may help you understand what I am about to say to you.

Some well-meaning Christian friends told us that God had nothing to do with the death of our son. They said that it was all Satan's work, that a loving God wouldn't do such a thing to us. Honestly, I believe they said that for their own benefit, not mine. They could not picture the kind of God that would allow this horrible thing to happen and not do anything to stop it. Theirs is not the God of the Bible. Besides, the thought of God losing control brings no comfort at all, only hopelessness.

Let us rewind the story for just a moment. It is the week of Christ's death and Peter has just proclaimed his willingness to follow Christ anywhere, even to death. Jesus says something very significant, "And the Lord said, Simon, Simon, behold, *Satan hath desired to have you, that he may sift you as wheat*: But I have prayed for thee, that thy faith fail not: and when thou art converted, strengthen thy brethren. And he said unto him, Lord, I am ready to go with thee, both into prison, and to death. And he said, I tell thee, Peter, the cock shall not crow this day, before that thou shalt thrice deny that thou knowest me" (Luke 22:31-34 KJV emphasis added). Did you hear that? Satan had asked permission to attack Peter, and it was granted! The same thing happened to a man named Job in the Old Testament. Satan asked permission to attack Job. God allowed Satan to kill Job's children and his servants. Satan took away all his wealth, and gave him a horrible disease. None of this could have happened without God's knowledge and His permission.

Jesus said Satan is a murderer and the father of lies. Satan exists. Anyone who refuses to accept this fact and live their life accordingly is a fool. Satan is an enemy of Christ and opposes Christians. He patiently probes for weaknesses and undermines our faith, hope, and love. Satan must be taken seriously but without being overtaken with terror, because Christ has defeated him. Satan is not a god. He is a created being, a fallen angel. He is powerful and cleaver, but has no more authority than allowed by God.

Attacks of Satan are permitted by God as well as limited by God. Satan is on a leash and God holds the end of that leash tightly. Peter was sifted like wheat, but his faith remained. Job was savagely attacked not once but twice and yet he endured. Both Peter and Job understood that God owns all things–even we are His by creation. As the Owner of all things, if He gives you a lot or a little, He has the right to decide. Everything and everyone He places in our life is His gift, but only for a time. We came into this world with nothing and we will leave everything behind when we leave. Everything we have is loaned to us by God. As the Owner of all things, if He decides to take back what belongs to Him; He has every right to do that. When He gives or He takes, He is doing nothing wrong, He is simply being the Owner, the Lord of all.

Living in America you will see affluence everywhere you look. Down the road from where I live are some houses that cost hundreds of thousands of dollars. There are cars advertised on TV nightly that cost tens of thousands of dollars. The stock market soars, and millions of dollars are made and lost in a day. It is all on loan, every bit of it. We own nothing forever. It all belonged to someone else before we were born, and it will all belong to someone else when we die. We don't even own our children. People belong to God. Children are given to us to take care of, love, teach, discipline, and encourage. Then we release them into the world to do the same thing with children that will be loaned to them.

When Job lost everything and stood by the ten freshly dug graves of his children, he said, "Naked came I out of my mother's womb, and naked shall I return thither: the Lord gave, and the Lord hath taken away; blessed be the name of the Lord" (Job 1:21). The Apostle Paul who spent much of his ministry in prison wrote to his young pastor friend Timothy, "For we brought nothing into this world, and it is certain we can carry nothing out. And having food and clothing let us be therewith content" (1 Timothy 6:7-8). We brought nothing in and we will take nothing out. Everything in between is on loan. God owns it all. If we can get to the place where we do not consider ourselves the sole owner of the Lord's property, we can more easily release it when the true Owner wants it back.

Satan is a creation of God and is a part of His plan. He uses Satan to accomplish what He wants. We are not capable of understanding all that He is doing around us. Knowing this does not help us to see our tragedy any clearer, but it does help you understand that God did not lose control. What happened may seem unfair and you are probably right. What happened to Job was unfair. What happened to Peter was unfair. What happened to Jesus was unfair. What happened to my family was unfair. Haven't you noticed the worst things always seem to happen to the best people, and the unfairness of it all?

But according to the Bible that's the way we think, not the way God thinks. He still has a plan. He has never lost control. He still loves you, even if you don't feel like it right now. Jim Elliot, a missionary who died at the hands of the Quichua Indians he went to help in South America wrote, "He is no fool who gives what he cannot keep to gain what he cannot lose." God will never lose you because He is always in control.

So how should we respond to what has happened? Job said this, "Shall we indeed accept good from God and not accept adversity?" (Job 2:10). Job answered the question with a question. This question is not asked for us to answer, but for us to ponder. Does God have the right to do whatever He thinks is best? Is He really God? This is an especially hard question for those who have believed the false promises of the health and wealth doctrine, those who think life owes them pleasantness and a trouble-free existence. We are still on this side of Heaven, and this means suffering, sickness, and death. But this does not mean hopelessness or helplessness, for there is still the sovereignty of God. An author once wrote that it is easier to lower our view of God than to raise the heights of our faith. God is totally, absolutely, and eternally in charge. If He gives you a blessing, He is in charge. If He takes away a blessing, He is in charge. Our choice is whether or not we will accept and submit to this truth and trust Him.

Brandon trusted God. He knew that he belonged to God. That is another reason I can continue. Brandon knew Jesus Christ as his Savior. Several years ago, just before Christmas, I asked everyone in our family to write their salvation testimony. I then took everyone's testimonies, made a book out of them, and gave everyone a copy of the book for Christmas. It was so very wonderful to read of everyone's assurance of their salvation. I still have Brandon's original hand-written copy of his testimony. In it he tells why he knew he would go to heaven when he died.

I also know Brandon's life was one of a child of God. After his death we went through his belongings. We looked through his computer and found nothing inappropriate. I read his E-mails and found one warning him to be careful. It seems he was helping the homeless; spending time with people close to the college that were living on the street.

He went to Trinidad to help build a church and do street evangelism. He wanted to be a doctor in a Spanish-speaking country and help people. He used to say he would probably be paid in chickens, preferably live ones. He knew. And he was sure of it.

I also know. I am sure of where I am going when I die. I know Jesus died for me on the cross and paid for my sin. God has adopted me as His child. I will one day go to heaven, not because I have done anything to deserve or earn it, but because I know Jesus, and I believe Him. I know that when I close my eyes on this earth and open them in heaven I will see someone I know. I will see Jesus. After I see Jesus I will see my son and my friend, Brandon. I know. I am sure. Jesus is alive.

Brandon in Trinidad pouring concrete at midnight

CHAPTER THREE

FAITH, FRIENDS, FINANCES, AND A FUNERAL

Simon Peter, Thomas (nicknamed "Twin"), Nathanael from Cana in Galilee, the brothers Zebedee, and two other disciples were together. Simon Peter announced, "I'm going fishing."The rest of them replied, "We're going with you." They went out and got in the boat. They caught nothing that night (John 21:2-3 The Message).

I can think of a lot of reasons they went fishing. They might have went fishing simply to occupy their minds, a type of sedative for their pain. Maybe they went to have some familiarity back in their lives, comfort in the midst of their confusion. Perhaps they went back to work because they needed some money. Someone once told me that Jesus and Satan were partners in the same waltz. Another way of saying it is, good things and bad things travel together and arrive at about the same time.

When Brandon was killed we had to go into a room filled with caskets. There we had to decide what price range we could afford to place his body in. We then had to sign a stack of papers with the word "deceased" next to our son's name. I wanted to go fishing instead.

We then had to go to the graveyard. There we filled out forms for a loan on a small piece of ground to call Brandon's grave. All these decisions and financial requirements come at the most difficult time in your life. I would rather have been fishing.

On top of everything else, a year earlier our church had gone through a split. The finances of our church were depleted, therefore some of my benefits were cut. There had been a decrease of people in our church and those who remained were doing more than they could handle. I started praying differently that year. Strangely, I had been asking God to send some men to our church to help me. I asked God specifically for guys like Simon Peter, Thomas, Nathanael, James, and John. That year He began sending them. When Brandon died, they were there. They have walked with me and even understood when I wanted to go fishing. When we pray we expect God to answer with something perfect. He often sends imperfect people in answer to our prayers.

Just take a look at the friends Jesus chose to surround Himself. Simon Peter was the closest friend Jesus had and he was constantly sticking his foot in his mouth. All through the Gospels we read, "and Peter answered..." when there are no questions asked. Peter always had an opinion–his own. Peter was a powerful man, physically, and strong in personality. Because of his profound statement of faith in Matthew 16:13-23, Jesus nicknamed him "the Rock". Five verses later because his profound statement of foolishness, Jesus calls him Satan. He said he was ready to go to prison and to death with Jesus. Jesus then said, "I tell you, Peter, the rooster will not crow this day before you will deny three times that you know me" (Luke 22:31-34).

Next is Thomas, or as he has been known for generations, "Doubting Thomas." After the resurrected Jesus had appeared to the other disciples they said to him, "We have seen the Lord." So [Thomas] said to them, "Unless I see in His hands the print of the nails, and put my finger into the print of the nails, and put my hand into His side, I will not believe" (John 20:24-25).

Nathanael (also called Bartholomew) was a bigot. Nathanael did not think too highly of the people from the other side of town. Philip came to Nathanael and told him they had found the Messiah from Nazareth. Nazareth was the side of town where the poor and the middle class lived. Nathanael said to Philip, "Can anything good come out of Nazareth?" (John 1:45-46).

James and John were double-trouble. They were sent to a group of people called the Samaritans to arrange for Jesus to minister to them. The Samaritans refused to let Jesus come, so when James and John learned of it they said, "Master, do you want us to call a bolt of lightning down out of the sky and incinerate them?" Jesus turned on them: "Of course not!" (Luke 9:54-55). Later, Jesus tells His disciples that He is about to be mocked, flogged, spit upon, crucified, and rise on the third day. James and John respond to this by saying to Jesus, "Teacher, we have something we want you to do for us." "What is it? I'll see what I can do" Jesus answers. "Arrange it," they said, "so that we will be awarded the highest places of honor in your glory—one of us at your right, the other at your left." (Mark 10:32-37).

There are two more problem children listed, but they are nameless in the Bible. Why? I believe the Holy Spirit did this so that one might be seen as possibly me. At times I am prideful, presumptuous, prejudiced, pushy, and pompous. Since Brandon's death I have been especially difficult. Before Brandon died I was very organized and efficient. I prided myself in my ability to see everything in black-and-white. I had very few gray areas in my life, and had little compassion for anyone who did. I did everything a certain way, thinking I knew most of the answers to life. As my organized life was blown apart, I couldn't organize all the pieces. Suddenly life wasn't so black-and-white. I blamed God. I got very angry at Him, and told Him so–often.

Some people told me to never question God. I asked them if they had ever read the Bible. The entire book of Psalms is filled with questions at God. The books of Job and Lamentations are filled with questions. I read where Jesus asked God why. (Matthew 27:46 The Message) "Around mid-afternoon Jesus groaned out of the depths, crying loudly, "Eli, Eli, lama sabachthani?" which means, "My God, my God, why have you abandoned me?"" God is big enough, and wise enough to deal with our questions. He hasn't answered all my questions. He has given me the assurance of knowing He loves me, even when I want to go fishing.

Take heart if you have days when you want to climb into the fishing boat, because you will be in some very good company. All those in the fishing boat in the Sea of Galilee finished well. While in Rome doing missionary work, Peter was arrested and kept in prison for nine months. He somehow escaped, but went back when his wife was arrested. His wife was executed. As she was led forth, Peter comforted her with the words, "Remember the Lord." Peter was executed also. Upon his own request, Peter was crucified head downwards. He felt unworthy to die in the same manner as Jesus. He preached from his cross until he died.

Thomas traveled to India as a missionary. There were many converts as a result of his preaching. He was preaching in Madras, India when he was told to stop preaching. When he refused to stop proclaiming his faith, he was stabbed with a lance.

Nathanael Bartholomew was a missionary to many countries. He left behind the Gospel of Matthew wherever he went. He was told to renounce his faith, but refused even when he was skinned alive. He died still proclaiming Jesus as the Lord.

James was the first apostolic martyr of the Christian faith. Herod III beheaded him. The accuser of James was so struck with his calm heroism that after speaking to James, he became a believer, and was executed on the same block freshly stained with the blood of James.

During the reign of Nero, John was brought to Rome. He was cast into a cauldron of boiling oil, but was miraculously preserved. After this ordeal he was imprisoned on the Island of Patmos. He died of old age in Ephesus. These men were not superhuman. They are not any different than us, they made mistakes, had doubts, and went fishing, but they did trust Jesus.

Even before Brandon died God knew what I would need after his death. My prayers were answered. He sent some men into my life at just the right time, and they trusted Jesus. Since that time the church has become financially stable. I have gotten my benefits back. We even remodeled the church the year after Brandon died. The men God had sent worked together.

If you have days when life becomes more than you can handle, and all you want to do is go fishing, look around and see if God has sent somebody to go with you. He has a plan for our lives. He wants you to finish well. You will, if you trust Him. Maybe today all He wants you to do is go fishing.

CHAPTER FOUR

OUR TOUGHEST BATTLES AREN'T WITH THE DEVIL
THEY ARE WITH GOD

Ron Landers sang in the bars of Michigan, drank a lot, and was overwhelmed with the responsibilities of having a mortgage, wife and kids. One night he went out for a drink and a drive and finally came to a stop in Anniston Alabama. He tried leaving his problems behind, got an apartment, a new job, and started singing in the bars of Anniston. But Ron was still miserable and looking for some hope. One Monday night a group from our church knocked on his door and asked him if he knew about a friend named Jesus. Ron was soon singing in the church about his new friend Jesus. Ron really wanted to go home to his wife and kids, but his wife didn't believe he had truly changed. Ron became a good friend and we prayed often about him going home.

Ron became a Christian music evangelist and was driving a truck when his vision became blurry. He sat across the doctor's desk and listened as the doctor explained how cancer can blur your vision. His first words were "Why, Lord?" His life was finally worth living. He was looking forward to years of successful ministry, and God allowed cancer to enter the picture. He had a brain tumor and was told he would have to go through a series of chemo treatments and eventually surgery. Ron would take his guitar to the waiting room and give concerts to others awaiting their turn for chemo treatments. One day he was singing and talking in the waiting room when a 75 year old man asked Ron how he could go to heaven. Ron told him about his friend Jesus.

Ron told me, "If the only reason I got a brain tumor was so I could lead this one man to Christ, it was worth it." The time came for Ron's surgery and they did another MRI, but couldn't find any trace of a tumor. Ron still sings about his friend Jesus in churches and waiting rooms.

The question of why is throughout the Bible. To be honest, the verses after that particular question often do not answer it. Why, God? Why me? Why now? Why this? Have you ever questioned God?   There are some who tried to tell me not to question God. They told me it's not right to get angry at God. They said God will never put more on you than you can bear. The Bible says you can be angry and sin not (Ephesians 4:26). So why can't you be angry at Him? I cannot find the verse in the Bible that says God won't put more on you than you can bear. I've looked for it. The Bible does say God's grace is sufficient for anything we are up against. That means God will sustain us in the circumstance. The Bible actually says that God will never allow more to be placed in our lives than He can bear for us. That's a big difference! He seems to believe we can withstand a lot more than we think we can. Here is were the battles begin. Why is God doing this?

"Simon Peter announced, "I'm going fishing." The rest of them replied, "We're going with you." They went out and got in the boat. They caught nothing that night. When the sun came up, Jesus was standing on the beach, but they didn't recognize him. Jesus spoke to them: "Good morning! Did you catch anything for breakfast?" They answered, "No"" (John 21:3-5 The Message). They had watched as Jesus was arrested. They had heard the news of His death and burial. Hiding from the authorities for fear they would be next, their

18

mourning was amplified with fear. Now, after finding Jesus had risen from the grave, their emotions were on a roller coaster ride. Why was all this happening? Why, Lord? So they decide to find some emotional comfort by going back to the way things used to be before they met Him. They went back to fishing.

You face another day without your loved one knowing you will be faced with what used to be normal, but now isn't. Nothing is normal. You dive into your old routines trying to feel what you used to feel, normal. You hear a song they liked or see a car like theirs. You look at the door they went out and never came through again, and you don't feel normal. All you feel is loss. The Bible says that loss is normal. There is a time for everything, even for loss to be normal. I confused normal with comfortable. I thought normal was a pain free and a simple life, but that is not what God promised. God promised that in the midst of all the pain and all the turmoil, He would never leave us. He promises to be in control no matter what has happened to disrupt our "normal" life. He promises that what has happened is not a mistake.

The will of God is always for the good and the blessing of His children even when His children do not understand. As a loving Father, He will make decisions that are beyond our understanding. He is wise, and He is loving. He is not making a mistake, no matter how it feels at the time.

I once stood at the grave of a little newborn girl and was asked to say something to comfort the family. That was the first time I had ever read this poem. In the valleys of life it is comforting to know God hasn't made a mistake. The poet A. M. Overton has so beautifully written about this:

He Maketh No Mistake

My Father's way may twist and turn,
My heart may throb and ache,
But in my soul I'm glad I know,
He maketh no mistake.
My cherished plans may go astray,
My hopes may fade away,
But still I'll trust my Lord to lead
For He doth know the way.
Tho' night be dark and it may seem
That day will never break;
I'll pin my faith, my all in Him,
He maketh no mistake.
There's so much now I cannot see,
My eyesight's far too dim;
But come what may, I'll simply trust
And leave it all to Him.
For by and by the mist will lift
And plain it all He'll make.
Through all the way, tho' dark to me,
He made not one mistake.

CHAPTER FIVE

DON'T JUST STAND THERE GUYS, PRAY SOMETHING!

(John 21:3-5 The Message) Simon Peter announced, "I'm going fishing." The rest of them replied, "We're going with you." They went out and got in the boat. They caught nothing that night. When the sun came up, Jesus was standing on the beach, but they didn't recognize him. Jesus spoke to them: "Good morning! Did you catch anything for breakfast?" They answered, "No."

Prayer is difficult when you are in the pit. Most of the time we have prayed for others when we see them in the pit, or we pray for God to keep us out of the pit. We pray about the pit. Everything changes when you are praying from the pit. The view is different, your point of view is difficult. It is different because you are attempting to see God through the circumstances, it is difficult because what you see is disturbing to you. You see a distorted view of God, distorted because you are attempting to focus through the tears.

When Brandon didn't come home after his girlfriend's curfew, we knew something was different, but not necessarily wrong. Brandon had a cell phone with him and we began calling him. There was no answer. We called his girlfriend's parents and found out he had left in time to be home by now. Still not getting an answer on his cell phone, I started calling the hospital emergency rooms, and we started praying. We prayed for God to protect our son. We pleaded with God to bring our son home safely. We asked God to be with him if he had been in an accident. We prayed...until the doorbell rang. The prayers we prayed were not answered the way we expected. We cast our net all night, and like the apostles, caught nothing. We had faith. We knew how to pray. We had prayed for others and witnessed miracles. We had given God the glory, and expected the same would happen for us. We believed God would do what we asked. Then the doorbell rang.

When people started arriving in our home and people started calling me, some wanted to pray with me. Their words were those of faith. But when I bowed my head and approached the throne of God, I was angry. I felt betrayed. I had prayed all night and had caught nothing. So why cast the net again? Being a preacher, I was careful who I told this fact to, but a wise child of God told me, "Don't worry, God's big enough to deal with your anger. Go ahead and be angry. It's proof you still believe. You have to believe in Him to be angry at Him." Don't get me wrong, I don't believe you should be disrespectful to God, but being angry can be the catalyst to help you find out what prayer really means.

Prayer is not telling God what to do. Prayer is getting in the presence of Truth. Prayer is not how you change God or necessarily change the circumstances. Prayer is how God changes us in the midst of the circumstances. Someone gave us a framed Scripture and because of where it is I look at these verses every day. The Scripture is Apostle Paul's words on prayer: (Philippians 4:6-9) "Be anxious for nothing; but in everything by prayer and supplication with thanksgiving let your requests be made known unto God. And the peace of God, which passeth all understanding, shall keep your hearts and minds through Christ Jesus. Finally, brethren, whatsoever things are true, whatsoever things are honest, whatsoever things are just, whatsoever things are pure, whatsoever things are lovely, whatsoever things are of good report; if there be any virtue, and if there be any praise, think on these things. Those things, which ye have both learned, and received, and heard, and seen in me, do: and the God of peace shall be with you."

Prayer is getting in God's presence to get God's perspective on the situation. It is deciding if you will trust Him with the results. Prayer is giving your request to God, and God giving you peace in return. How can you have this peace? By thinking the way Paul speaks of here. Seeing things truthfully and honestly. Expecting justice, purity, and loveliness. Believing the good report, thinking virtuously, and praiseworthily. Only God can give you this kind of peace. As this verse says, peace in anxious times "passeth all understanding." How can this happen? This way of thinking requires one thing–the Holy Spirit! The Holy Spirit will produce this thought process if you allow Him. The God of peace will be with you.

(John 21:6 The Message) "[Jesus] said, "Throw the net off the right side of the boat and see what happens." They did what he said. All of a sudden there were so many fish in it, they weren't strong enough to pull it in." Praying means you aren't quitting. Prayer is refusing to give up. Prayer is confessing to God you don't have anywhere else to go. Nobody else has any answers. No one can give you peace. You can pray through the tears. You can pray through the anger. You can pray through your doubt. Prayer does not mean God will necessarily change the situation, but He can change you in the midst of the situation. Prayer means God will use whatever is available to help you through.

Pray as God's child. Then your Heavenly Father will send His children to come to your aid. That is what happened to us. God sent some of His children, our brothers and sisters in Christ to help us. Prayer is seeking comfort and strength from God. This is often brought by others and given to you. He will send family, neighbors, coworkers, and your church family to help. Nothing helps like caring people simply being near you.

So many came around us and cried with us, hugged us, and brought much needed friendship. Our church family surrounded us, answered our phone, brought food, and encouraged us. Brandon's funeral was the day following our twin daughters' birthday, and our friends gave our daughters a much needed birthday party when we couldn't. One lady that owned a cleaning service came and quietly cleaned our house. Ladies sat in our bedroom with my wife as she faced the first night without our son. Men came and sat in our carport well into the night–simply letting me know they were there if I needed them. So many came and answered our prayers for help. That is one reason we pray, because God will send help.

The day Brandon was killed was the most difficult day I have ever experienced. Yet at the same time, it was the day my Christian family revealed the love of Christ like no one ever had before. Romans 8:26-27 tells us the Holy Spirit prays for us even when we don't know how to pray, "Likewise the Spirit also helpeth our infirmities: for we know not what we should pray for as we ought: but the Spirit itself maketh intercession for us with groanings which cannot be uttered. And he that searcheth the hearts knoweth what is the mind of the Spirit, because he maketh intercession for the saints according to the will of God."

When you pray, expect Him to answer in a very present and personal way. Expect your Heavenly Father to trust some of His children with your need. When we got home after going to the morgue I shampooed the carpet. The State Troopers had mud on their shoes and they had gotten it on our floors. I was in shock after seeing Brandon on a steel table covered with a sheet. I had to do something to occupy my mind, or I would have gone insane. So I started shampooing carpet. Soon my friends arrived and offered to help me, but allowed me to continue. They knew I needed to stay busy. When I finished the floor some helped me make a list of everyone who needed to be called. Then they let me make the calls. They offered to make the calls for me, but supported me when I needed to make the call myself. This is how prayers are answered: God sends people to comfort you however you need comfort. I believe one of the things He is doing is sending the answer to your prayers through His people.

While the dirt was still fresh on my son's grave, I stood there and prayed. My cell phone rang and when I answered it a minister I used to serve with was on the line. He was in South Carolina on a mission trip. He said God had just spoken to him and told him to call me. He asked me if I was having a hard day. Only God could do that. Only God could hear one of His children in Alabama ask for help and at the same time speak to another of His children in South Carolina. Only God could tell him to call me and answer my prayer.

In the same context, not long ago, I was working when God impressed on my heart to call a pastor friend of mine. He had recently experienced a divorce. I was extremely busy and argued with God for a moment, but I gave in and called. My friend answered his phone and began to get choked up. He told me he had just prayed and asked God to have someone come by or call him because he was having a very tough day. Then his phone rang. Only God can do that.

When God impresses you to call, then call, and answer a prayer. I often tell people that God has some truly wonderful children. He has some that really care and will help. May God use you to help one of His children who is praying.

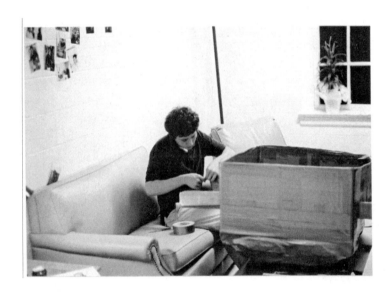

CHAPTER SIX

DOUBT IS FAITH'S COMPANION

Brandon built a boat out of empty water bottles, duct-tape, and cardboard. He sailed it in the fountain at the center of Samford University the last day of his freshman year. He was sailing some previously uncharted waters until campus security came to conclude his voyage. He had discovered how to enter many of the locked buildings on campus at night and was giving "tours" to some of his closest friends. He had two young ladies that called themselves 'John and Paul', secret admirers that had noticed him at a freshman party. They started leaving him notes in a cookbook in the college library. They kept him in the dark about their identity for weeks. They finally met him at a coffee shop and became close friends. He did things like this a lot. He would get a look in his eye and you would know he was embarking on a new adventure.

Brandon was not only my son, he was my friend. When he was ripped away my life became unraveled. I had already planned how I was going to do his wedding. I looked forward to sitting at my dinner table and talking to a daughter-in-law. Brandon was going to college to be a medical missionary. I was so anxious for him to walk across the stage and receive his diploma. I looked forward to spoiling his children and being there when they were born. The future I knew was one filled with my Brandon. When you lose a loved one, you not only lose a person, but you lose everything that person would ever do. You lose everything that person would ever bring into your life. You lose more than just a loved one; you lose the future as you knew it. You face a future you have never planned for. This is confusing and frightening. The only hope you have is in God, for He knows your future.

"Then the disciple Jesus loved said to Peter, "It's the Master!" When Simon Peter realized that it was the Master, he threw on some clothes, for he was stripped for work, and dove into the sea. The other disciples came in by boat for they weren't far from land, a hundred yards or so, pulling along the net full of fish. When they got out of the boat, they saw a fire laid, with fish and bread cooking on it" (John 21:7-9 The Message). The disciple Jesus loved is John. When John told Peter "It's the Master!", Peter jumped. If you lost someone and the chance to see them again occurred you would jump, too.

Peter knew he wouldn't be growing old alongside Jesus. His plans and his dreams were gone. Now he had to establish new plans, dream new dreams, and do it without his loved one by his side. He never imagined his life would have turned out like this. The future, as he knew it, was gone. His faith had to move forward, but Jesus' footprints had been beside his for some time now. Suddenly there is only one set of prints in this journey. Jesus would continue to be with Peter, just as He has, and will be with anyone who has lost a loved one. Peter now had to live by faith, not by sight. Life is different than you expected. Life is still livable despite the loss, because He is still with you in the journey. The pain of loss remains, but you move forward by faith in the company of the Lord.

When sorrow consumes your thoughts, you find it almost impossible to remember the goodness and the grace of God. The more intense the pain, the more difficult it is to find peace. In these moments you need your faith the most, you find it almost impossible to appropriate. It is so easy to forget God's grace in these difficult times. That is why we have a small piece of duct-tape covered cardboard on a table in our living room. It is a reminder, a piece of a boat built to sail in the waters of adventure. It reminds me that Brandon had given his life to Christ and was going to sail anywhere God wanted him to go. Brandon believed in the grace of God, and this small piece of "the boat" reminds me of that. You will never forget the loss of your loved one. You will heal and move forward, and memorials help along the way. Reminders can be something as simple as a poem or a photo album reminding you of God's blessed gift. It doesn't matter how you remember the grace and the goodness of God but it is important that you do.

Our plans may be disrupted, but God's grace is always sufficient. Grace is often defined as God's unmerited favor. I often say grace is God supplying for His child anything that is required from His child. He gives us what we need. He always has and He always will give you what you need when you need it. Realize that without the possibility of failure, there can be no faith. Doubt is the companion of faith. Faith is continuing the journey, eventually getting through your doubt. Peter had doubted, but given the opportunity, he jumped. He decided to go through the doubt and get to Jesus. Remember that, when you begin to doubt, and jump, or build a boat out of cardboard, duct-tape, and water bottles. Go sail some uncharted waters.

Brandon's completed "boat"

CHAPTER SEVEN

THE GOD YOU CANNOT SEE CAN BE RECOGNIZED

I once heard someone say losing their loved one was like living with an amputation. You miss them every day. There is an empty place where they are supposed be. But you must learn how to live with the loss. There will come a moment when you realize you have a choice and you decide to continue. This is the beginning of healing and rehabilitation. This time is different for every person. Although you will never "get over it" you can go on.

In the midst of the normal happenings of life, you suddenly realize you are not living in a way defined by your loss. You are living life as a result of your loss. Life is no longer "normal" so you must make the conscious choice to find a "new normal." Living after the loss means being with people who may or may not understand. It means allowing them to love you and allowing yourself to love them in return.

"When they got out of the boat, they saw a fire laid, with fish and bread cooking on it. Jesus said, "Bring some of the fish you've just caught." Simon Peter joined them and pulled the net to shore—153 big fish! And even with all those fish, the net didn't rip. Jesus said, "Breakfast is ready." Not one of the disciples dared ask, "Who are you?" They knew it was the Master. Jesus then took the bread and gave it to them. He did the same with the fish. This was now the third time Jesus had shown himself alive to the disciples since being raised from the dead" (John 21:9-14 The Message). In the verses before us, when Jesus comes and meets with the apostles, He offers no explanations. He simply fixes breakfast and gives it to them. Much can be learned by what is not in the Bible. The Bible does not attempt to explain God, it simply proclaims God's existence. In Genesis 1:1 there is no explanation of where God came from or what His plans were when He created everything. The Bible is void of many explanations, especially those dealing with the question of suffering.

When suffering arrives, so do friends. When you are laying in the hospital, dismissed from a job or staring down at divorce papers. When you are listening to your unwed daughter tell you of her decision to keep the baby. While you are standing in the graveyard and reading a loved one's name on the tombstone, distressed and bewildered. You are suddenly alone, so people start showing up to help. The problems arise when they feel they have to tell you exactly what is wrong and what must be done to fix it. Suffering attracts those who want to fix you. They arrive with their answers to your problems (just read the book of Job and listen to his friends). Often they use the Word of God, but use it very loosely. They believe there must be a spiritual diagnosis. There must be a heavenly prescription that you can take that will make you all better. It sounds helpful and hopeful but it often isn't. There probably aren't any words that will help, for there is no explanation to what just happened to you and is causing you to suffer.

There is a lot of teaching now on being "healthy, wealthy, and happy". This propaganda says that if you live a certain way and believe a certain amount, you will be exempt from suffering. This teaching does not stand up to the examples given in the Bible. There are those who try and tell you that everything is going to be alright. You simply have to think a certain way and say the faith-filled words. They are simply trying to provide a glib explanation to a complicated circumstance. They are putting a band-aid on a compound fracture and ignoring the resulting complications.

Note that Jesus gives no clichés of positive thinking nor is there any spiritual small talk. Jesus just fixes breakfast and sits down to eat with them. No one asked for an explanation and one wasn't given. Jesus had died, was now here and would soon leave again. They would be left to live after their loss no matter how much they wanted Him to stay. Real faith cannot be merchandised or reduced to a success story. True faith is simply refined in the fires and storms of pain and loss, and more often than not, without any explanation. We hate to see people suffer. We desperately want to help prevent, or alleviate the suffering. This is compassion. It is a good thing, but we really must be careful not be presume too much. Do not attempt to fix everything today. Don't explain how to have the perfect marriage, the best children, or normal mental health by comparing it to your life. No matter how insightful you are, you do not really know why this happened. You do not understand the full impact of this on the suffering person. Besides, the sufferer will not get over this today no matter what you say.

Truthfully, most of the time, people do not suffer less when they are committed to following God. They actually suffer more. This suffering, according to the Word of God, has the potential to deepen their faith and strengthen their relationship with the Lord. It can reveal the grace of God to others. It can help others in the days to come, but while it is happening, it just hurts.

Instead of observing the suffering from the outside and throwing in the occasional well thought-out lifeline, why not enter the suffering with them. Go to them with no explanations, no answers, and no expectations. Be with them as much as you are able. Stop looking down at them and trying to raise them up. Look up to them and try to learn something from them. Join them in their protests and also in their prayers. Share their suffering and their submission. Fix them some breakfast and sit down to eat it with them–quietly.

We have a lot of information at our fingertips. At incredible speed we simply type our question into the search box and press Enter. The search engine will reply with hundreds of options and responses. It is hard for a twenty-first century Christian to accept the fact that some things are not to be known. We have book stores full of Christian books on every topic imaginable. We have seminaries offering courses on every doctrine of the Bible. Many of us have highlighted our Bibles so we can maneuver through the pages of Scripture to answer all of life's toughest questions. Life seldom turns out as expected, and confusion always leads to questions. Suffering brings us one step deeper into the mysteries of God. As His light is revealed in our darkness we see more clearly and we struggle less. We learn how He speaks to us through the pain and the suffering. This is how you live through the loss. God begins to fill the void. He doesn't fill the void with simple answers. He fills the void with Himself.

CHAPTER EIGHT

SILENCE IS GOLDEN...AND A LOT LESS PAINFUL

After walking away from the well-meaning person in the parking lot, I knew they meant no harm. What she had said was well intentioned, but it left me very hurt and angry. I told my wife that one day I would write a book on what not to say to someone that has lost a loved one. Although this is not a book on what not to say, this is just a chapter on watching what you say. I hope it will help you know that people say some very strange and sometimes hurtful things. Just love them for their attempt to help. It is very difficult to know what to say. I have said some pretty stupid stuff myself, but I'm learning the art of silence.

Jesus told a parable about the impact of loss. In this parable He emphasized the importance of the individual. Jesus said, "Suppose one of you had a hundred sheep and lost one. Wouldn't you leave the ninety-nine in the wilderness and go after the lost one until you found it? When found, you can be sure you would put it across your shoulders, rejoicing, and when you got home call in your friends and neighbors, saying, 'Celebrate with me! I've found my lost sheep!' Count on it—there's more joy in heaven over one sinner's rescued life than over ninety-nine good people in no need of rescue. Or imagine a woman who has ten coins and loses one. Won't she light a lamp and scour the house, looking in every nook and cranny until she finds it? And when she finds it you can be sure she'll call her friends and neighbors: 'Celebrate with me! I found my lost coin!'" (Luke 15:4-9 The Message).

"Just be thankful that you have other children" is one the sayings people have said to us. In the parable Jesus emphasized the importance of one no matter how many others there are. This is true of sheep, coins, and loved ones. Even though we have other children, this fact in no way lessens the fact we have lost one.

The first Sunday after the funeral we went to church and someone came up to me and said, "I know how you feel. My dog was hit by a car yesterday and I had to bury it." I smiled and thanked this person and asked them if they were doing alright.

To help us feel better about our son being taken away another saying we have heard often is apparently a very old saying. Someone told me they thought it was part of an old gospel song. It goes like this: "God only picks the best flowers to add to His garden in heaven." Does that mean the rest of us that remain are not good enough to be put in this celestial bouquet? I also do not believe our son is in heaven as a display or as an ornament.

Because God knows the future, some have told us that perhaps God took Brandon away before he did something that would have caused him to deny his faith. Some have said God could have taken our son before he became a drug-addict or an alcoholic. If that is true, why do any of us remain? We all fail in some way. We all sin, and God leaves us here to continue. He leaves us here as proof of His grace.

Another often-heard phrase is that our son is in a better place. This is why we are not supposed to be so sad. They said our son wants us to get over this and go on with life. I know my son is in heaven and I look forward to being there myself. I am homesick for a place I have never been, but I still miss him no matter where he is. We did not lose our son. We know exactly where he is.

I was sad when he went away to college. I missed him when he was at Samford. I was sad because his room was empty, and there was an empty place at the table, even though I knew he would be home every weekend. There is still an empty place at the table, and he is not going to come through the door this weekend. He will never come to me. I have to go to him. I miss him terribly, no matter how much better the place where he is might be.

Remember, it is not our responsibility to explain to people how they need to feel or how they should respond to the loss of a loved one. Please do not think I do not want people to speak to me, nor do I scrutinize everything people say to me. I need to talk. I need to talk to people about my pain. I want people to talk to me. I just hope they do not feel they are responsible for explaining my loss or helping me to understand my loss. I will probably never understand my loss until the day the Lord explains it to me. And on that day, when we are reunited with our loved ones, I hope you will celebrate with me like the parable says we will.

"It is better to go to a house of mourning than to go to a house of feasting, for death is the destiny of every man; the living should take this to heart" (Ecclesiastes 7:2 NIV). One definition of the word sympathy is "a relationship between persons or things wherein whatever affects one similarly affects the other." Martin Luther King, Jr. said it this way, "True sympathy is the personal concern which demands the giving of one's soul." To help someone in grief, to express meaningful sympathy means we will help carry their sorrow, and feel their grief as Jesus did for us, "Surely he hath borne our griefs, and carried our sorrows: yet we did esteem him stricken, smitten of God, and afflicted" (Isaiah 53:4). How do we do that?

First, express your own grief. Do not be afraid you will add to their own sorrow. You will actually help validate it. They will realize their loss has affected others. Grief is comforted by tears more than answers or reasons.

Second, do not be afraid to talk about the person who died. Mention the good things you remember. Share special moments that the loved one might not know about. Doing this confirms that the person's grief is legitimate. Not only have they lost a loved one, the world has lost a good person. They have a valid reason to be sad, and to grieve. Acknowledge their pain, do not minimize it. Assure them that their pain is legitimate.

Third, offer to do something specific. This is the "carry your sorrows" part. Carrying their sorrows usually involves a sacrifice more than just signing your name to the bottom of a card. With a little creativity you will think of some meaningful action to take. Brandon's funeral was on July third. Our daughter's birthday is July second so we were not in the "birthday party" mood. As I mentioned before some ladies from the church threw our daughters a party. They showed up with gifts, cake, ice cream, and gave our daughters the party they needed at that time. They came, and carried our sorrows.

CHAPTER NINE

THE EMPTY TOMB DOESN'T QUIET
THE CROWING ROOSTER

At my son's funeral I spoke of making a mistake in his life: I blinked. One minute his pudgy little hand was wrapped around my finger, and when I blinked his hand was holding a steering wheel. At the conclusion of that service a young man who knew Brandon came to me and asked how he could have what Brandon had, a real relationship with God. He accepted Christ as his Savior as they were taking my son's body to the graveyard. Someone asked me a question later. Did I think that young man's salvation was one of the reasons God allowed Brandon to die? I don't know. I have to admit that if God had given me the option of that young man's salvation and my son living, I would have chosen my son's life. That may not sound very "spiritual". I do feel grateful that God was glorified at that service, but I also believe God is big enough that He could have saved that young man somewhere other than at my son's funeral.

Once again the possible answer to the why question seems less than satisfactory. God asks tough questions but He never asks a question in order to gain information, He is omnipotent. He asks questions to reveal truth to us. I guess that's why Jesus didn't ask Peter why. He didn't ask Peter why there had been three denials or why Peter had decided to go back to his old way of life. I want to ask God why, but I'm glad He doesn't ask me. He asks a totally different question.

His question doesn't deal with the past and its mistakes, rather He asks a question on how to deal with right now, how to make it through today. After breakfast, Jesus said to Simon Peter, "Simon, son of Jonah, do you love me more than these?" "Yes, Master, you know I love you." Jesus said, "Feed my lambs." He then asked a second time, "Simon, son of Jonah, do you love me?" "Yes, Master, you know I love you." Jesus said, "Shepherd my sheep." Then he said it a third time: "Simon, son of Jonah, do you love me?" Peter was upset that he asked for the third time, "Do you love me?" so he answered, "Master, you know everything there is to know. You've got to know that I love you." Jesus said, "Feed my sheep." (John 21:15-17 The Message).

Jesus didn't ask Peter about his failures, but neither did He ask him about his triumphs. He didn't ask Peter about walking on water. He didn't ask him about being nicknamed "The Rock" or about being one of the "inner three." Peter, James, and John were the three on the Mount of Transfiguration. Peter was one of the three taken into the bedroom of Jarius' daughter when Jesus raised her from the dead. Peter was one of the three taken closest to Him while Jesus prayed in the Garden of Gethsemane. Jesus didn't bring up Peter's triumphs, for they were fleeting. Jesus didn't bring up Peter's failures, for these were fleeting too. The only thing that lasts is love, and that was the question. And Jesus didn't ask this question to get information. As Peter said, Jesus knows everything. He asked Peter a question so Peter could find an answer.

We all must have this conversation with Jesus sooner or later. We have to sit before Him, allowing our hearts to be examined by the Savior and finding the answer to the most important question of life. Do I love Jesus unconditionally? That is the word for love Jesus uses here, agape. Agape means unbounded, unrestricted love. Is this how we love Jesus, no matter what? No matter what has happened in the days leading up to this question, regardless of what we understand. No matter what we have seen or heard, do we still love Jesus?

While the sound of the rooster's crowing was still ringing in Peter's ear, Jesus loved Peter. Jesus loves Peter, no matter what has happened. Peter denied knowing Jesus, not just once, but three times. Peter was not at the cross with Jesus. Peter wasn't at the temple preaching about the resurrection of Jesus. He went fishing instead.

The empty tomb didn't eliminate the crowing rooster so he went back to his old ways of cursing, crying, and fishing. Jesus still has a place for people like Peter. Some have been with Jesus, and He saved them, but they have yet to stop and know His love. We must wait, be still, and be loved by Him. This is especially true in times when our lives are in turmoil. Maybe you need to take time to do that right now. Just get alone with

Jesus and tell Him if you've doubted. Tell Him if you've cursed, cried, and went fishing. Tell Him you're scared and angry. He will listen, and then He will ask you, "Do you still love Me?"

Brandon in his Samford dorm room

CHAPTER TEN

HE SIMPLY TURNED AND WALKED OUTSIDE OUR DOOR

Again we said, "Be careful!" as you darted out the door
Not realizing we would not be seeing or hearing you any more
Your excitement was so evident as you hurried toward your
date
If only we had known the reality of your fate

The grip of fear crushed us in the night as the doorbell rang
The Trooper's solemn faces, the harsh reality, the intense pain
That night we changed, son, for part of us was taken
Savagely ripped from our hearts leaving us broken and shaken

We strain through the silence to hear your voice from an empty
room
We speak words to some flowers, some dirt, and a marker at
your tomb
We miss you so much, son, life seems impossible to bear
Others do not understand our empty hearts, our empty tears,
and our empty stare

We remember how we prayed to have a son just like we had
Your life filled with so much good and so little of anything we
saw as bad
Your desire to be a missionary even when you were so small
Surrendering to God your life, your love, your future, your all

Remembering how you spoke so intelligently even before you
were one
Your incredible ability to think, yet with such a desire to have
so much fun

Always on your next adventure, looking for the next big thing
to do
Where's that laugh, that look, those many experiences that we
know as you?
You always said, "I'm a good boy" or "The Favorite" and you
are a wonderful son
Not rebellious or mean, but just enough mystery to keep things
fun
You made work enjoyable and school and adventure for so
many others
A best friend, a close companion, a boyfriend, even an
"adopted brother"

The guys called you Stompy*, to your girlfriend you were
Lindo**
So carefully you chose those who looked through your life's
window
You had seen life's hypocrisy and solidly refused to join in
So those who really knew you, fell in love with one incredible
friend

We want you to know, our only son, our friend, our love
That we know you are with your Savior, your Lord up above
And we can't wait to see you again one day, reunited in the
sky
But until then, please understand as we so often pause and cry

You are our son and we are so very proud of you
A gentleman, a scholar, a friend, one of very few
Our young man with so much to give, and so very much to live
for
Our son who simply turned and walked outside our door

*Brandon had a cockroach he named "Stompy" while at Samford. His college friends started calling him by his pet's name
**Lindo is Spanish for "Beautiful"

My wife and I wrote this poem after Brandon's death attempting to put into words what our hearts were feeling. This poem and a scrapbook filled with glimpses of his life are on a table in our living room as a way of keeping his presence in our home. This is not a shrine or a memorial as much as it is our family's remembrance table. This is important for us right now. It is a place in our home where we see him. We can take time to look back with deep love into his time with us, and look forward with deep longing to when we will see him again.

CHAPTER ELEVEN

DOES JESUS HAVE FAITH IN YOU?

Service is the echo of the call. The call of God is not to service but rather to love. "Do you love Me?" The call is to love. The echo of that call is our service, "Feed My lambs, Shepherd My sheep, Feed My sheep." The Garden of Gethsemane was the place of surrender for Christ. These words were Peter's Gethsemane, his own personal place to surrender to the Lordship of Jesus Christ. Peter was already dead when the Apostle John wrote this, so what is written about Peter's future had already happened. Jesus restored Peter so He could lead Peter. Peter's life would echo the call.

"I'm telling you the very truth now: When you were young you dressed yourself and went wherever you wished, but when you get old you'll have to stretch out your hands while someone else dresses you and takes you where you don't want to go." He said this to hint at the kind of death by which Peter would glorify God. And then he commanded, "Follow me."" (John 21:18-19 The Message). There will be days ahead when you will have to go on, even though you don't want to. You will carry the pain of loss along the remaining road of your life. Others have told you that "time heals all wounds" but your burden is lessened only slightly, and at times seems overwhelming.

So you meet with Jesus, for He promised to help you with your burden. Jesus said, "Are you tired? Worn out? Burned out on religion? Come to me. Get away with me and you'll recover your life. I'll show you how to take a real rest. Walk with me and work with me— watch how I do it. Learn the unforced rhythms of grace.

I won't lay anything heavy or ill-fitting on you. Keep company with me and you'll learn to live freely and lightly"(Matthew 11:28-30 The Message). Don't just believe in Jesus, believe what He says, trust Him. Read His words again and again, but slowly and thoughtfully.

He will lift you up, and He will give you strength to continue. He is not speaking here of merely physical weariness, but emotional and spiritual weariness also. Your soul can become exhausted, and no amount of physical rest or no change of scenery helps. Jesus stands a little taller than you do. When He is in the yoke, He takes most of the burden. He is a lot stronger than you. When He is in the yoke, He walks with ease. But you must enter this yoke with Him and let your steps be in rhythm with His. This is not something hard to do. It is simply trusting Him, and being aware of His presence. Tell Him you will walk with Him, and you need His companionship in this journey. Shift your focus from living without someone to living with Jesus every moment of every day. Echo His call, "Yes, I do love You, Jesus."

One hopeful thing about grief, you can live through it. As humans we have a lot in common because God has made us in His image. What you are going through is what others have, are, and will go through until Christ returns.

In the days, months, and years to come you will experience shock, struggle, survival, and strength you never thought you could possess.[1]

- SHOCK: The First 12 Hours After Profound Loss

God's grace kicks in and sustains you. I once got my thumb caught inside a machine I was working on and my thumb was crushed. The problem was, I had to disassemble the machine to get my thumb out. But through the entire ordeal my thumb never hurt...until I got to the emergency room. The entire time I was working to remove my injured thumb I felt no pain. You understand how physical shock enables you to be protected from intense pain during the initial moments of trauma to your physical body. This also happens to your mind. It is an equally real and merciful thing that happens to protect you from overwhelming events. Numbness arrives with horrible news. It is your mind's way of protecting you. This happens naturally when your emotions overload, and your mind short-circuits. You gradually come out of this state as the intense pain of reality arrives at full force.

- STRUGGLE: The First 12 Weeks After Profound Loss

Each day is unfocused. You have to go on living. You wish you could quit the life you have been given

---

[1] This information is from some notes I have on counseling. I believe the original thought was derived from a bookmark by "Life Action Ministries" (www.lifeaction.org).

and get your old life back. Moments of denial rush into your thoughts. You want to believe that it didn't really happen. You hope it is simply a bad dream, and you will wake up and everything will be just like it used to be. This is normal as long as these desires do not continue into the future.

Anger rages into your day. Too often the handiest people to vent this anger on are those closest to you. Venomous words hiss from your mouth in ways you have never experienced before. Recognize the very human urge to lash out and realize what it can cause. When this anger is turned inward, it becomes bitterness which births depression and guilt. The only way to deal with this is talking. You must talk about what you are feeling to someone that cares and wants to help you understand. Ignore those who just want you to "get over it." They want things to get back to normal. They want you to be like you used to be around them. They are uncomfortable with the situation and want it to go away. They try to tell you to be strong and get back to life. You may make them uneasy when you want to reveal the reality that it could happen to anybody, even them. Express your feelings, talk them out while remembering to give yourself some grace. Be patient with yourself and ask others to be patient with you. Your emotions may need some time to simply pause, to hang an "Out To Lunch" sign on your day. Let people help you. Don't be afraid to ask for some help. Get some support. Even though everything in you says to be "self-sufficient", let others help you. Keep reminding yourself, when you feel you are imposing on others, that if the situation were reversed you would be looking for an opportunity to provide love and support to help them.

Loneliness, in the middle of the crowds trying to console you, is normal. This is a journey you will take solo. Nobody else is exactly like you. Nobody else can completely understand what you are feeling or thinking. Nobody else grieves like you. We are all unique, and there is a factor of loneliness to that. Be as nice as you can to those who are trying to help. Even to those who will say, "I know how you feel," or "I thought you would be over this by now." They do not have a clue, and there is no use trying to explain it to them.

Desires vanish and things just don't matter any more. The things you once valued do not hold the importance they once did. Your appetites vanish–food, sleep, relationships, hobbies, and work. You have a one-track mind. You cannot understand why everyone else is continuing to laugh, eat, sleep, and play when this incredible loss has occurred. But it did not happen to them in the same way it happened to you. You still have a hard time with a world that continues without seeming to remember the life-crushing event that has altered your life forever.

One of the most unrealistic beliefs during these days is that you are in complete control and behaving like you once did. You are wandering around in a daze, and your mind is not functioning correctly. Be careful resuming "normal" activities and do not expect them to be "normal." You will forget things. You will be unable to remember simple information you have used for years, but relax, you are not going crazy. Catastrophic loss is like the amputation of a limb. You will never get over the loss, but you can learn to live with the loss. There must be adaptation, acceptance, and a relearning of how to do simple things that you once took for granted. Continuing on does not mean you are forgetting the loss, nor are you ignoring the loss. You are simply learning to survive with the reality of the loss. This requires patience and practice, but it can be accomplished through faith, endurance, and lots of prayer.

- SURVIVAL: The First 12 Months After Profound Loss

Anniversaries, birthdays, holidays, vacations, family portraits, and just about anything else will never be the same again. Just when you get through one, another comes rushing at you. Do whatever it takes to survive. Do what you have to do to take care of yourself. The more you are able to talk about it the less the pain will overwhelm you.

You will suddenly get stuck doing things that seem more important that they really are. You will believe things have to be done a certain way. Any other time, you wouldn't have cared how it was done. This is hyper-focusing. It will diminish naturally as time progresses and your priorities become more rational. Your challenge is to understand what is mental confusion and what is reality. Having a sense of humor and allowing yourself to laugh during this time will help you. It will also lessen the likelihood of becoming unfair to others.

During these days you will find it hard to deal with God. Your relationship with God has just changed forever and your confidence in Him. Your faith is being stretched to the limit and questioned. There is anger at God for allowing this to happen. His love for you is questioned. He sat and watched this thing happen, and this makes you very angry. Anger toward God is especially difficult for many people tell us we are not to question God, or be angry at Him. They would really be shocked if they knew what you were really thinking right now! You are torn between being honest and having faith. You are having trouble praying and reading the Bible like you once did. You will beg God to be what you want Him to be, but He is not our image of Him, He is much bigger and cannot be placed within a safe, comfortable little box of beliefs. Realize this, God is big enough to handle your anger and your doubt. Be honest with Him. He knows what you are feeling and thinking anyway, so why not tell Him? You will pray again, but differently. You will read your Bible again, but with deeper understanding and intimacy.

Seek good Christian counseling. Why do I specify good Christian counseling? Because there is some bad Christian counseling. Why Christian counseling? Because that is the only kind that will give you a way through. Secular counseling will take you to a place, a person, or a problem to place blame. You can point at it and say, "There is the reason I am like I am!" That only gives you something to blame. You need more than that. You need Someone to help you forgive, adjust, and live with your loss. Christian counseling will help you understand why you are feeling the way you feel. Then it will help you go from where you are to where Jesus can help you. The only true source of wisdom is God, and a Christian counselor will be led by the Mighty Counselor.

• STRENGTH: The First 12 Years of Grief

Memories of the first hours, days, weeks, and months are often remembered, often flooding in and overwhelming you. You are amazed that anyone could continue to live with part of their life torn from them. The question of survival is answered slowly. The hands on the clock keep moving no matter how you feel. The moments of intense pain will still be with you. A sound, a smell, a sight will bring back the first moment you received the news and will buckle your knees. Gracefully these moments will grow farther and farther apart. You have survived the trauma. There were and still are moments you believe you won't survive, but you have and you will. Eventually you will learn to laugh again, just as you have learned to live and love again, only differently.

Jesus said in John 16:20-22 (The Message), "Then fix this firmly in your minds: You're going to be in deep mourning while the godless world throws a party. You'll be sad, very sad, but your sadness will develop into gladness. When a woman gives birth, she has a hard time, there's no getting around it. But when the baby is born, there is joy in the birth. This new life in the world wipes out memory of the pain. The sadness you have right now is similar to that pain, but the coming joy is also similar. When I see you again, you'll be full of joy, and it will be a joy no one can rob from you." Believe Him. Place the truth of Scripture into your mind and your heart. This seed will produce hope in your life. Life will bring its challenges, but Jesus will walk with us through any and all valleys no matter how deep, dark, or long. Trust Him, walk with Him, love Him unconditionally. Remain close to Him regardless of what happens. He will lead you through, even in the middle of the night.

CHAPTER TWELVE

SEARCHING FOR THE SACRED
ONE DAY AT A TIME

When the doorbell rang one of the things I held most sacred was lost, my family as I knew it. I considered my family sacred. Webster defines sacred as, "Set apart for a holy purpose, religious." People had told us for years that our son was set apart for a holy purpose because he was so evangelistic. He had wisdom beyond his years. He determined very early to be set apart to be a missionary doctor, and help people. I am a pastor, and my family is very religious. I considered that sacred.

When my family unit was ripped, I began searching for the sacred. I thought that sacred meant safe, not vulnerable to destruction. In my search God took me to a section of Scripture where two disciples are also searching for the sacred. The thing they considered most sacred had been destroyed, or so they thought. They considered their Messiah to be sacred. They had followed Him and accepted Him as set apart for a holy purpose, religious. And then they saw Him murdered and buried. Their next move was to go to a place called Emmaus. (Luke 24:13 The Message) "That same day two of them were walking to the village Emmaus, about seven miles out of Jerusalem." What was in Emmaus? It doesn't say. I also went searching for my Emmaus. I wanted to find a place where I might restore the sacred in my life. Maybe you are looking for your Emmaus. Perhaps you want to find a place where the loss of the sacred might make sense.

I am on that journey myself. In this journey I have learned a couple of things. One, you cannot lose what is truly sacred. Anything that is sacred, or set aside for God, belongs to God. Anyone that belongs to God is eternally protected by Him. I did not lose a son, I know exactly where he is right now. Two, along the journey you will find the truth while searching for the sacred. The sacred belongs to God, not us. The sacred is set aside for God's use and His pleasure, not ours. We do not own what is truly sacred, we simply have access to it for a period of time.

This is my journey to Emmaus. This is a daily walk, a quiet time with God that is divided into one day journeys. A quiet time is a journey, a walk with God to a desired destination. Colossians 2:6 states, "As ye have therefore received Christ Jesus the Lord, so **walk** ye in Him." Since we are saved through faith (Ephesians 2:8), it is required we also must walk or live by faith. Faith is what changes our spiritual perception. Walking by faith is not easy, just as it was for the disciples on the road to Emmaus after they had suffered their incredible loss.

We used to have a treadmill. A treadmill is a machine which enables you to walk at various speeds and various inclines to produce a desired result, namely exhaustion and sweat. The thing most noticeable about this grueling endeavor is that no matter how hard or how long you walk, you never actually go anywhere. This is how I would have described my walk with God after the death of my son. I achieved a lot of exhaustion and sweat but did not go very far. I became concerned that I was destined to go through this life like I was trudging on a perpetual "nowhere machine". One of the hardest things I tried to do was have a consistent quiet time with God. Hopefully this will help you get started.

In our text, we find that there are two disciples traveling together on the road to Emmaus. We find out in verse 18 that one's name is Cleopas, but the other's name is never mentioned. It is not mentioned if this follower of Christ is a man or a woman. Perhaps this is for a purpose, so you can place yourself in this Scripture. These two disciples were sad. They had witnessed Jesus' death and burial. They mourned and wept. Their minds are filled with questions and confusion about the last few days. They are also concerned about the future. Maybe you have traveled this road yourself. Take a look at what happens in their lives after the death of their loved one. See from the Scriptures how Jesus deals with their mourning. Allow God to teach you how to make your own journey in search of the sacred. Using your sanctified imagination, imagine that this is you traveling a dusty road on that strange Sunday afternoon. While taking this journey, please remember one very important thing. He is alive, trust Him.

DAY ONE

CONTINUING TO WALK WHILE THE PAIN
CONTINUES
John 14:27-31 The Message

"Jesus said, " I'm leaving you well and whole. That's my parting gift to you. Peace. I don't leave you the way you're used to being left—feeling abandoned, bereft. So don't be upset. Don't be distraught. You've heard me tell you, 'I'm going away, and I'm coming back.' If you loved me, you would be glad that I'm on my way to the Father because the Father is the goal and purpose of my life. I've told you this ahead of time, before it happens, so that when it does happen, the confirmation will deepen your belief in me. I'll not be talking with you much more like this because the chief of this godless world is about to attack. But don't worry—he has nothing on me, no claim on me. But so the world might know how thoroughly I love the Father, I am carrying out my Father's instructions right down to the last detail. Get up. Let's go. It's time to leave here."

Before we start our journey, please allow me to give you a small bit of advice. The Scripture for today has meant a lot to me. Take a moment to read it very slowly. Someone said to me "time heals all wounds". I decided not to tell him he was so very wrong. My wound has yet to heal. The other day I spoke to a man that had lost his son over twenty years ago. He told me not a day goes by that he doesn't hurt for his son. Every week I go to a graveyard. I look down at the markers that have my father's name, my brother's name and my son's name on them. I saw my father die in the hospital after battling a long disease. He had battled a disease most of my life.

We were sort of "prepared" for his death, if you can really prepare for a loved one's death. My brother died at work of a heart attack. My brother's death was a shock. My son's death was also a terrible shock. We were unprepared for either of them to die. Prepared or not, a loved one's death is difficult. I don't have the answer to the pain, nor do I know any shortcuts through the valley. All I can tell you is not to give up. Keep going whether you feel like it or not. Continue your journey one step at a time. Trust in God's grace.

Remember there are still temptations to be overcome. Satan has not ceased his activity even though you may feel too weak to fight. There will be opportunities to give into temptations. Keep your guard up. If you have lost a spouse, there will be temptations to fill that void with someone else. If your loss has left you financially challenged, there will be temptations to find the quickest and easiest way out.

If you are like me, there may be the desire for revenge. Be careful. Even though Brandon was totally innocent in the crash, the drunk driver only received twelve months probation and counseling. I thought this was nothing more than a slap on the wrist. I wanted him to pay for what he had done. By the grace of God I didn't pursue revenge, I found forgiveness. Believe me, I didn't forgive him because I wanted to. I forgave him because I found I needed to. After a very long and agonizing struggle, I gave the situation over to God. I am still trusting Him with the results. This did not happen over night. For me, forgiveness was a process, and a temptation.

If you have a teenager who has lost a loved one expect the thoughts and feelings of the teen to be amplified, contradictory, and inconsistent. When they invite you, talk honestly with them and listen. Offer to help them find support that may not include you. The teen will feel unrealistically responsible for the loss. They often feel vulnerable to death themselves. They may exhibit defensive behavior to cover up their grief. They may even become reckless with their own life to prove they are not vulnerable. They may spend periods of constant activity or total inactivity. They may become sleepless or spend prolonged time sleeping. Expect and tolerate certain inconsistencies without allowing them to endanger themselves or others.

Trust in the Lord with all your soul and with all your strength. Allow God to heal you and to use you to help others, when it is time. We will be spending a lot more time there than here, so don't give up. Eternity is coming and one day we will stand before the Lord. He will answer our questions and wipe our tears. But until that day, don't quit, don't give up. Keep going on through the pain. He is alive, trust Him.

Pray: Lord, I come to you broken and bleeding inside. Only You can reach those areas and begin my healing. Increase my belief in Your ability to intervene supernaturally and do the impossible. Thank You, Lord. Amen.

DAY TWO

WHEN MAKING PLANS, CONSIDER GOD
Luke 24:13-14 The Message

"That same day two of them were walking to the village Emmaus, about seven miles out of Jerusalem. They were deep in conversation, going over all these things that had happened."

Each day we do not know how long we might stay, nor do we know where God might take us. You can never plan for God. You can prepare yourself for what He is about to do with you. Our plans and His plans are seldom the same. God is actively working in our lives to bring us to Himself. Our plans are based completely on our understanding of the facts. The facts as far as the two on the road to Emmaus understood them were:

- Jesus was crucified Friday morning. He was dead and buried in Joseph's garden tomb.
- Jesus' ministry was over. The apostles were frightened fugitives hiding inside an upper room.
- They had heard rumors about Jesus' tomb being empty. It is impossible for the dead to get out of a grave.

The facts as far as the two on the road understood them were not true.

My wife, daughters, and I were in Florida the week before Brandon died. Brandon remained home to work, and spend time with some of his friends. Our vacation plans did not include coming home early, but a hurricane arrived. I believe God sent the hurricane so we would go home. We watched the weather grow

60

progressively worse and made the decision to leave. If we had not left early we would not have gotten to spend any time with Brandon before he died. We returned home on Sunday afternoon and ate dinner with Brandon. We all said goodbye to him as he left for his date. The hurricane came just in time.

On the way home from Florida we were deep in conversation, going over all these things that had happened. We were a little upset our plans had been altered. We did not know at the time why we were going home so early. We were later glad we did. The two on the road to Emmaus were discussing the problems they had encountered. They talked of how their plans had been altered, and what their plans were. The problem was, they did not know all the facts.

The half-brother of Jesus spoke of making plans in this way, "And now I have a word for you who brashly announce, 'Today—at the latest, tomorrow—we're off to such and such a city for the year. We're going to start a business and make a lot of money.' You don't know the first thing about tomorrow. You're nothing but a wisp of fog, catching a brief bit of sun before disappearing. Instead, make it a habit to say, 'If the Master wills it and we're still alive, we'll do this or that.' As it is, you are full of your grandiose selves. All such vaunting self-importance is evil. In fact, if you know the right thing to do and don't do it, that, for you, is evil." (James 4:13-17 The Message). James was saying that our plans and God's plans are seldom the same. Consider that God may alter your plans at any moment. Trust Him when He does. He knows all the facts as they truly are. God knows the course of the day. He knows the distance we can travel, and the directions we should go to accomplish His will for our lives. James tells us that this life goes by quickly. We can miss God along the way if we are too wrapped up in ourselves. We must stop and look for Him or at least consider Him.

Consider God as you begin this journey. Consider that He knows the truth about all the facts. He also knows the truth about us. His desire for you in this journey is for you to know Him better. Remember, His plans are the best plans for you. Trust Him no matter what you feel or what you understand right now. He is alive, Trust Him.

Pray: Lord, help me to seek You before getting physically involved in Your work for the day. Thank You, Lord. Amen.

DAY THREE

IS IT WELL WITH MY SOUL?
Luke 24:15-16 The Message
"In the middle of their talk and questions, Jesus came up and walked along with them. But they were not able to recognize who he was."

Jesus came up and began walking with them, but they did not recognize Him. You must be looking for Him to see Him. God's activity is all around us, yet we miss so much of it. Sometimes the pain blurs our perception of His presence when we take the first step of the journey. We love to hear how God sends those unexpected checks in the mail at just the last minute. None of us want to be in the financial disaster required to need the check. We all clap and shout when we hear testimonies of the doctor not being able to find that tumor after the church prayed the Sunday before the surgery. None of us want to sit in the doctor's office and hear him tell us we have cancer. In those moments it is incredibly difficult to see God. It is so very easy to miss His presence in the beginning of the journey.

Our dear friend David Valenzuela played his guitar and sang "It Is Well With My Soul" at Brandon's funeral. It was a moving experience, but made even more meaningful when you know the story behind the song. This song was written by a man who understood loss to an incredible depth. He was able to put his feelings into words.

This hymn was written by Horatio G. Spafford, a business man from Chicago. As a young man Spafford had established a successful legal practice in Chicago. He

63

had invested heavily in real estate on the shore of Lake Michigan, and the Chicago Fire of 1871 wiped him out financially.

He enjoyed a close relationship with evangelist D. L. Moody. He decided to assist Moody in one of his evangelistic campaigns in Great Britain. This would provide a time of rest for his wife and four daughters. Because of some last minute business developments, he was detained. He sent his wife and girls ahead on the S.S. Ville du Havre. On November 22 the ship was struck by the Lochearn, an English vessel, and sank in twelve minutes. His daughters were among those lost at sea. His wife cabled her husband, "Saved alone". Spafford left by ship to join his grieving wife. On the sea near the area where his four daughters had drowned, Spafford penned these words.

When peace, like a river, attendeth my way, when sorrows like sea billows roll–whatever my lot, Thou hast taught me to say, It is well, it is well with my soul.

Tho Satan should buffet, tho trials should come, let this blest assurance control, that Christ hath regarded my helpless estate, and hath shed His own blood for my soul.

My sin–O the bliss of this glorious tho't–my sin not in part, but the whole, is nailed to the cross, and I hear it no more: Praise the Lord, praise the Lord, O my soul!

And, Lord, haste the day when my faith shall be sight, the clouds be rolled back as a scroll: the trump shall resound and the Lord shall descend, "Even so"–it is well with my soul.

It is well with my soul, it is well, it is well with my soul.[2]

It is evidence of the grace of God that Spafford does not dwell on his sorrow and trial. He focuses on the salvation and the return of Christ. If Jesus is alive and returning, you have the hope of seeing your loved ones again. This is why it is well with your soul. Jesus is alive. In the middle of our questions, He comes up and walks along with us. In the impossible situations He walks up beside us. He quietly accompanies us along the way. When you can only see the circumstances, He comes along and helps you to refocus. He wants you to keep your eyes on Him. Even when you do not yet see Him, He is there. We will know Him in a way we have never known Him before, if we look for Him. Look for Him today, He is nearer than you think. He is alive, Trust Him.

Pray: Lord, I will not be self-sufficient. Help me remain aware of my need for help from You and others. Thank You, Lord. Amen.

---

[2] Spafford, Horatio G.: It Is Well With My Soul. The Baptist Hymnal, Convention Press, Nashville, Tennessee. 1991. Page 410

DAY FOUR

WHEN GOD ASKS QUESTIONS
Luke 24:15-17 The Message

"In the middle of their talk and questions, Jesus came up and walked along with them. But they were not able to recognize who he was. He asked, "What's this you're discussing so intently as you walk along?" They just stood there, long-faced, like they had lost their best friend."

We tend to want to be blessed more than we want to be used by God. Do not dwell on how God can bless you. Look how He is wanting to use you. When you are used by God you are sure to be blessed. We search for comfort, He is searching for character in us He can use. We want to see God bless our families. God wants to use our families. We pray for God to bless our churches. God is calling out for our churches to be used by Him. The blessing comes when we are usable by Him. Jesus asked them what they were talking about. He wanted to know why they were sad along their journey. Jesus never asks a question for Himself. He asks questions to get us to thinking. He already knows all the answers, we do not.

My family has long discussions about the question of "Why?" We have discussed our belief in a God that would do this. We have talked much about the very existence of this type of God. Our whole world has been turned upside-down. I can imagine what the two on the road were discussing and their questions. They must have been asking how such a thing could have happened. They probable asked why God would allow the destruction of Jesus' ministry, and the ending of His life.

In the midst of the confusion Jesus asks them a question. His questions probe into the depth of faith, especially when our situations seem to be out of control. Sometimes we have days that seem "larger than life". We find ourselves surrounded by a storm of circumstances. The Holy Spirit led me to some Scripture that describes one day when Jesus had a "larger than life" day.

John the Baptist was His cousin and friend. John was a prophet who truly understood who Jesus was. John is brutally murdered. He is beheaded for telling the truth to Herod who then sends word he wants to talk to Jesus, too. John's disciples had come to Jesus with this horrible news. They were also looking to Him for leadership. The book of Mark tells us that at the same time the apostles Jesus sent out to evangelize had come back. They reported exuberantly of miracles. Jesus listened to bubbling testimonies of ordinary fishermen, tax collectors, and laborers who had witnessed the power of God. As the disciples of John and His own apostles are competing for His attention, 5,000 men with their women and children surround Him. Jesus wants some time alone to mourn the loss of His friend. He also wants to help His apostles keep their priorities right. He gets into a fishing boat and heads for the other side of the sea. When they get to the other side, the 5,000 men with their women and children are waiting. They had ran ahead of Him. They wanted Him to meet their needs regardless of how bad His day has been. Jesus calmly sits, and teaches them. He then feeds them all with a few loaves and a couple of fish.

How did He handle this "larger than life" day? The next few verses in the book of Matthew show us. The next few days we will take a break in our journey to see how to have peace in the center of a storm. This truth has carried me more days than I can tell you. I hope it helps you. What is a STORM? An acrostic is, Situations That Overwhelm Religious Methods. In the midst of the storm, relying on religious methods won't cut it. A shallow, or occasional religious activity is not a strong enough foundation when the storm comes. Going to church will not keep you from giving up, but it helps. A storm will overwhelm religious methods. A storm will not overwhelm a love relationship with Jesus Christ.

Storms come when you least expect them. As I stated earlier, there was a hurricane when we came home the day before Brandon died. It arrived in full force the night he was killed. The storm came while the State Troopers were pulling up in our driveway. The storm ravaged our peaceful home without warning, but not without grace. There really can be peace beyond our understanding in the midst of the storm. He is alive, Trust Him.

Pray: Lord, I am in a storm. In this time of crisis I trust in You to give me peace. Please keep me safe in Your mercy. Thank You, Lord. Amen.

DAY FIVE

TRUST HIS PROVIDENCE IN THE STORM
Matthew 14:22 The Message

"As soon as the meal was finished, he insisted that the disciples get in the boat and go on ahead to the other side while he dismissed the people."

His purpose is what brought me here. Crisis is conceived in heaven and birthed on earth. Faith has become a subject we discuss and a verse we quote more than the way we walk. Our misconceptions do not lie in the circumstances, but rather in the will of God. The question asked here is, "Would my God lead me into this storm?" The answer is yes, He did.

The verse says Jesus "insisted" that the disciples get in the boat and go on. The word in the original Greek means "to compel out of necessity." This implies that it was necessary for the disciples to get into the boat and go out into the sea. Remembering that Jesus is God, there is also the realization that He knew there was a storm coming. It was a really big and scary storm. What was the necessity for the disciples to get into what will soon become a water-filled, storm-tossed boat? Could the answer be to find peace? Yes, peace is exactly the reason He insisted.

God often has to insist, otherwise we would not get in or go on. He knows the outcome. We only know about the storm. While going through our storm people told us God "had nothing to do with it." They assured us that God "would not put more on us than we could stand." None of this counsel helped us because none of this advice was true. In the storm, remember that His purpose has brought you here. He is in control and He has a purpose for this.

The apostles were still in the will of God, yet were headed into a terrible storm. Not every bad circumstance you find yourself in is the judgment of God or punishment for something you did wrong. These apostles were completely innocent in all of this. They were totally obedient to the exact will of God yet were sent into a terrible storm.

It is so very easy to play the "what if" game in the storm. What if we had done this differently? What if I had not done that? We second guess ourselves, and wonder why we got into the boat in the first place. When facing a storm our first instinct is to attempt to retreat. We want to go back and change something to stop the storm. To understand grace we must understand Lordship. Jesus put you in the boat, He is the Lord. Submit to His Lordship by trusting Him and not second-guessing Him. Don't look back and long for the shore when the winds begin to blow. Remember this truth: The will of God will never lead you where the grace of God cannot sustain you. Wherever He leads you He will sustain you.

They must have realized He purposely sent His closest friends into a storm while remaining safely on the shore. When the storm comes, there is always some conversation taking place. Remember Luke 24:13-14? "That same day two of them were walking to the village Emmaus, about seven miles out of Jerusalem. They were deep in conversation, going over all these things that had happened." Much of the conversation deals with how to get out of the storm. We calculate how to lessen the storm. We search for a way we can avoid the storm altogether next time. This type of conversation misses the point; His purpose brought me here. If He sent you into the storm, to get out would result in leaving His will for your life. Peace is found when we accept the storm as His will. He is God. He is your God, and He is God of the storms. He will not allow the storm to keep His will from happening.

Note in the verse that Jesus told them to go on ahead "to the other side." This is His promise in His providence. You will make it to the other side. He will see to it that you make it to the place He has sent you. He will get you through the storm, He will get you to the other side. You have His word on that. He is alive, Trust Him.

Pray: Lord, help my first response to be prayer when I become anxious about my circumstances. Thank You, Lord. Amen.

DAY SIX

SEEK HIS EMPHASIS IN THE STORM
Matthew 14:23 The Message

With the crowd dispersed, he climbed the mountain so he could be by himself and pray. He stayed there alone, late into the night.

His prayers will protect me here. He is praying for you by name in heaven. His prayers are probably not like most of our prayers. His emphasis is on the spiritual, not on the physical. We pray for symptom removal. We pray "feed me, clothe me, and make me happy." We pray for God to change the situation and make our life simpler. We associate comfort with peace.

Jesus doesn't pray for a change in the situation until there is a change in the saint. He prays for us to seek His face instead of His hand. We pray for welfare and He prays for worship. He prays for us to meet with Him to get His perception of the situation. His disciples never asked how to preach, heal, or raise the dead. They did ask Jesus to teach them to pray. They knew Jesus was a man of intense prayer and He prayed often. Prayer is our lifeline to God in times such as these, so pray often. If your situation is desperate, make sure you have desperate prayers. God will guide you through the dark valley you are in. Be honest with God about how you feel, your fears, and your desires. If our prayers are not honest, they are not prayers.

When Brandon was killed I questioned prayer. Before entering the storm I considered prayer like a blank check. God signed it and I filled it in. I prayed for God to do this, for God to stop that, and for God to be ready for my next desire. I prayed with faith. I did not realize my faith was in my ability to pray, not in the One to whom I was praying. Prayer was a way of using the Almighty to manipulate the world to my liking. Prayer was getting things my way. Prayer was giving God a piece of my mind. Then the storm came. I prayed, and things did not go my way, and my mind went to pieces. That is why I questioned prayer. It wasn't that I was questioning Biblical prayer, I was questioning my way of praying. If prayer did not allow me to get things my way, what was it for? If praying didn't stop the storm, why pray?

God has shown me that prayer is listening as well as speaking. When we are still and listen closely, we can hear what He is saying to us. When we hear what is on His mind we have the choice to obey Him or discount His directions. True, unrushed prayer is seeking the will of God. Praying is making His desires our own so that He can give us the desires of our hearts. Prayer is entering into the reality of God or it is not prayer. I have learned praying protects my mind from accepting the wisdom of the world. Prayer protects my emotions from the roller coaster ride of the storm. Prayer protects my will from choosing the wrong path in my confusion. There is a battle for our minds in the storm. Prayer helps keep our mind clear and our heart peaceful even when the storm rages.

Praying will keep your emotions from going haywire. Jesus told a story about a storm in the Sermon On The Mount. "These words I speak to you are not incidental additions to your life, homeowner improvements to your standard of living. They are foundational words, words to build a life on. If you work these words into your life, you are like a smart carpenter who built his house on solid rock. Rain poured down, the river flooded, a tornado hit—but nothing moved that house. It was fixed to the rock. But if you just use my words in Bible studies and don't work them into your life, you are like a stupid carpenter who built his house on the sandy beach. When a storm rolled in and the waves came up, it collapsed like a house of cards" (Matthew 7:24-27 The Message). The storms hit both houses, but only one collapsed. The one that stood the storm was the one believing and applying the truths of God. The one that crumbled was refusing to believe the truths of God. Prayer helps you to believe and then apply the truth of God to you life. Prayer gives you strength and stability in the storm.

Praying will help you make better decisions. You can know His will, but only if you believe what He tells you. God wants to give you His perspective. Prayer helps you to hear Him clearly in the storm. Jesus is still praying for you. He knows about the storm and He cares. He will bring you peace when you pray. He is alive, Trust Him.

Pray: Lord, I have a personal relationship with You. I want to walk in a spirit of humility, as Jesus walked, and live in recognition that You know about my storms. Help me to hear You, Lord. Amen.

DAY SEVEN

FEEL HIS ASSURANCE IN THE STORM
Matthew 14:24-27 The Message

Meanwhile, the boat was far out to sea when the wind came up against them and they were battered by the waves. At about four o'clock in the morning, Jesus came toward them walking on the water. They were scared out of their wits. "A ghost!" they said, crying out in terror. But Jesus was quick to comfort them. "Courage, it's me. Don't be afraid."

His presence comes to me here. He seems to wait until the last possible moment to arrive. When He arrives, He is seldom what we expect. Be assured, He always arrives. They were far out to sea. The wind was against them, and they were being battered by the waves. These rugged fishermen had been fighting this storm for hours, until four o'clock in the morning. They were exhausted, and had not yet reached the other side. The storm was not showing any signs of weakening. Can failure be in the will of God?

They had not succeeded in reaching the other side. This seems to be a failure. God's idea of success is not accomplishing a task. Success is not reaching the end of a journey, but rather how you get there. Success is remaining in the center of God's will without giving up. They failed to reach the other side, but they were not meant to get there alone. They were right were they were supposed to be, no matter how hard they had tried to reach the other side. We often feel like we have failed in the midst of a storm. The storm rages, we have toiled through the night, and we are still far from the shore.

Once again, success is not in reaching the other side. Success in the middle of the storm is continuing to do what God told you to do before you entered the storm. His presence comes to you here. My beautiful and charming wife has an enlarged concern (you will notice I did not use the words "fear" or "worry" for these can be interpreted as sin) about tornadoes. When the weather alerts sound and the local weather man counsels everyone to find a safe place to hide, she gathers her family like a mother hen gathers her chicks and herds everyone into the basement. Personally, I would rather stand outside and watch this incredible act of nature. In her delightful way, she assures me that if I am going to be dumb I had better be tough. On one particularly stormy day the warnings went off, and down we went to the basement. I stepped outside to see what all the commotion was about. Our daughters squealed for their father to come back inside with them and hide in the hallway. As I sat in the floor of our basement, I knew storms can be lengthy, boring events so I started playing a game with my girls. Soon our daughters were laughing as this terrible storm raged outside. Why? Daddy was there to protect them. As long as daddy is calm, the kids are calm. Kids do not analyze the dangers of the storm. They look around to see if anybody else is worried.

Our heavenly Father has never called an emergency worry session in heaven when storms arrive on this earth. He comes to stay with us in the storm. He allows us to act like His kids. This is where our peace comes from, His presence in the storm. In the storm Jesus came to them walking on the water. He was telling them to have courage and not to be afraid because He was there.

Often the hardest test is in our strongest subject. These men were seasoned fishermen. Fishermen are good sailors, and successful boatmen. Their life was lived on the water. In this storm they were very afraid. The water they were so accustomed to was suddenly overtaking them. They were good at getting their boats to the shore. This time Jesus told them to get there, and it proved to be impossible. If you look very closely, the deep, raging water that frightened them was under Jesus' feet. Jesus was walking on the thing that was threatening their existence, and fueled their fear. He was the Master of the water. They would soon see He is Master of the storm as well. He is the Master in your storm. He will come to you here. When He arrives, look very closely. The thing or the situation that frightens you most will be under His feet. He is still the Master of the storm.

Listen closely and you will hear Him. He is not saying you have failed. He is not telling you to try harder. He will come in the midst of your storm to give you courage. He will walk in your storm to remove your fear. Go ahead and act like a kid. Take a moment to notice Who is in your storm. He is alive, Trust Him.

Pray: Lord, thank You that the things that frighten me most are already under Your feet. Your are victorious over all things destructive. You are the Master of this storm. Thank You, Lord. Amen

DAY EIGHT

ENJOY HIS COMFORT IN THE STORM
Matthew 14:28-32 The Message

Peter, suddenly bold, said, "Master, if it's really you, call me to come to you on the water." He said, "Come ahead." Jumping out of the boat, Peter walked on the water to Jesus. But when he looked down at the waves churning beneath his feet, he lost his nerve and started to sink. He cried, "Master, save me!" Jesus didn't hesitate. He reached down and grabbed his hand. Then he said, "Faint-heart, what got into you?" The two of them climbed into the boat, and the wind died down.

His power will sustain me here. We must be willing to leave the "security" of our storm-tossed, water-filled boat to walk where Jesus walks. He wants us to walk with Him in the storm. He wants you to stand above your fears. But let me warn you to be careful what you say to God in your storm. He may hold you to it. Look to see where He is walking. Ask to join Him then climb out of your boat today.

Peter is the only person in history besides Jesus to walk on the sea. It was a short walk because when he took his eyes off Jesus he lost his footing. He ceased to walk and started to sink the moment the waves held his attention more than Christ. Peter was walking in uncharted territory. With each step he was moving farther from the boat. When you lose a loved one, you will have to walk in unfamiliar places with each step taking you farther from the comfort of your water-filled, storm-tossed comfort zone. Learn a very important lesson from Peter. Keep believing Christ will sustain you here.

I meet with a man a couple of times a month and we have "lunch with Jesus." We pray and talk about our walk with the Lord. He is a very godly man and I treasure our times together. Not long ago I was telling him of my desire to escape. I wanted to get out from under the pressures of the life God had given me. He looked me in the eye and said, "My friend, you are a slave of the wrong master." I didn't need to escape, I needed to surrender.

He asked me if I was trying to be the perfect pastor that could please my church. I answered yes. He told me I was enslaved to a church. He then asked me if I was trying to be a husband and father that fulfills my family's every need. I answered that I was. He told me I was a prisoner to my family. As we spoke I began to see that I had my eyes on all the tasks around me to the point I was sinking in them.

Jesus wants us to walk in unbridled freedom above our fears. That is where He walks. We become enslaved to the things we believe will hold us up. Anything other than Jesus will enslave us. We then begin to sink. Does this mean we shouldn't be involved in church, or be married and have families? That's absurd. Our chief purpose in life is to serve God. We are to please Him with our lives. When our focus is on pleasing Him, all the other things we worry about will fall into place. We have His word on that (please read Matthew 6:24-34).

How can we bring peace to others when there is so much conflict in our hearts? There was a conflict between what I was preaching and what I lived. There was a conflict between what I was and what I knew I could be. I was preaching of setting captives free while my own heart was in the grip of so many attachments, anxieties, and guilt. I was trying to father my children while harboring bitterness and resentment for losing my son. I was trying to give others a passion for the truth while stubbornly holding to my own views. I was enslaved and discouraged. I was trying to walk on the water with my eyes on the waves. Not until I cried out to Him did I regain perspective and stop sinking.

Let me encourage you to do three things. (1) Be honest about your feelings with someone you can trust and has godly wisdom. (2) Cry out to God when you feel yourself sinking in your circumstances. (3) Notice where Jesus is walking each day. Join Him by faith, no matter where He is.

There is incredible freedom in no longer having to have your own way. You will never be what others expect you to be. Stop trying to do everything others want you to do. Jesus tells us to seek first the kingdom of God and His righteousness and all these other things will be added unto us. Hold Him to His word. Step out of the prison of a storm-tossed boat and walk in the freedom of the waves where Jesus is walking. He is alive, Trust Him.

Pray: Lord, thank You for making me free. Please allow me the friendship of someone I can trust and has godly wisdom. Help me to join You where You are today. Thank You, Lord. Amen.

DAY NINE

FULFILL HIS EXPECTATIONS IN THE STORM
Matthew 14:33-34 The Message

The disciples in the boat, having watched the whole thing, worshiped Jesus, saying, "This is it! You are God's Son for sure!"
On return, they beached the boat at Gennesaret.

His promise assures me here. When Moses asked God what His name was, God answered with, "I AM". He did not say, "I Was" or "I Will Be." God is in the present tense. So many people only speak of what God has done in the past or what He will do in the future. Our testimony of God should be what He is doing in our lives right now. Now is all we have. If we are to walk where He walks we must give up living in the past, rehashing our regrets. We have seen losses, failures, and mistakes. We all have handicaps. Every person I know has missed opportunities. Bad experiences happen every day. We must begin to see the will of God in everything. All these things have worked together to bring us where we are today. Today is where you are with God.

When the storms of life hit, we want to live in the past. Life was simpler, or so we thought. We look back, wishing we could change something so that we wouldn't be in the storm right now. We live in the "what-if's" seeking to curb the pain of the present. God commands us to live in the present. Living the "I AM" way of life. He wants us to be assured of His grace today. You cannot go back.

The disciples saw Jesus in a way they had never seen Him before. This resulted in them worshiped Him even before they reached the other side. Worship, love, faith, and hope are always in the present tense. We cannot live in the past. Yesterday is a simply a memory. You cannot live in the past, worship in the past, love in the past, have faith, or hope in the past. If we cling to the past we will miss what is being revealed to us in the present. Worship Jesus today. Love Him right now. Have faith in Him now.

Faith is not living in the future, either. The future is a dream, a hope, a desire, a promise that is not reality yet. We cannot live in the future except in our minds. God expects us to have a faith that lives, a faith that works right now. Faith is not trusting Him yesterday or tomorrow, it is trusting Him today.

When life is hard and our faith is taking a beating, it is easy to believe we will get back to trusting God like we used to. We will walk with Him one day, and our faith will grow to greater heights than ever before, someday. We postpone true worship with our excuses of the past. We promise to live by faith with our intentions of the future. What does God expect of us today? He expects us to believe in Him where we are right now.

We lost our son to a young man's evil act because we live in a world filled with evil. Questions always arise toward God when you suffer because of evil. God seems to be absent from our pain. It seems God doesn't respond in our time schedule, but our view of time does not match God's. The real challenge for us is to continue living in the present, taking one step at a time. Even when it appears that evil has won. There are many Bible verses that deal with getting the proper view on life regardless of our circumstances.

At Brandon's funeral we played the song "I Can Only Imagine" by Mercy Me. It speaks of being in the presence of God in Heaven and imagining what type of response we will have. As the words filled the sanctuary, my wife's hands lifted toward heaven in worship. At her only son's funeral she worshiped. She later stated she tried not to, but in the presence of God she simply responded. In the midst of her storm Jesus came to her and she worshiped Him.

Worship Him with what you have right now. Worship Him as much as you can where you are. These men were still in the middle of the sea, miles from shore in a water-filled boat. They didn't wait until they were on the shore. They responded right where they were with what they knew, "This is it! You are God's Son for sure!" Do you know for sure today? Is He God's Son in your life right now? If He is, then worship Him. He is alive, Trust Him.

Pray: Lord, I do not understand all the things that have happened lately. Regardless of my understanding, I want to worship. Praise You, Lord for being my Savior God. Thank You for Your grace. Amen.

DAY TEN

THY WILL BE DONE IN HEAVEN...
Luke 24:18 The Message
"Then one of them, his name was Cleopas, said, "Are you the only one in Jerusalem who hasn't heard what's happened during the last few days?"

Cleopas asks Jesus if He truly understands the situation. We do the same thing with God. We go to Him and ask if He really understands what is going on in our life. We treat Him as if the situation has taken Him by surprise. We feel the need to inform Him of our situation. Cleopas thinks God has lost contact with reality. In this journey, hold to the truth that everything is right in heaven, and nothing has taken God by surprise.

We spend so much of our lives worrying about the circumstances. We trust so much in our apparent ability to control the situation, we forget that the control center of the universe is in heaven. We never know all the facts, nor do we completely understand the facts we know. We assume too much, over-speculate some, and anticipate the rest. Like the two walking to Emmaus, we are mostly confused about the situation, so we begin thinking God is confused about our situation. God is the only one who knows, understands, and controls everything. Do not become overwhelmed by what's happened during the last few days. Believe that God is in control.

I answered the phone and heard the quivering voice of a friend of our family. I had been attempting to call her and she was returning my call. We had played "phone tag", alternately leaving one another voice mails.

I told her I had been praying for her because God had placed her on my mind. She said she was having a particularly difficult week and thanked me for praying. She had recently lost her husband in an auto accident, and had lost her son a few years earlier in an auto accident. We have our grief and God's grace in common.

She was telling me of some bittersweet memories and we began talking about our loved ones in heaven. We were attempting to narrow the gap between the living and the departed. I told her I did something that I'm not sure most people would find theologically accurate. We are commanded not to pray to angels or dead loved ones. We also know that those who had a relationship with Jesus on this earth are in His presence after their death. We are also told to ask anything of our Lord. We have no problem asking Him to do things for us, so sometimes when I pray I ask Jesus to tell Brandon that I miss him, and I love him. I believe Brandon is in heaven with Christ. I also believe Christ hears and answers my prayers. I think Jesus can do something for us in heaven just as He can do anything on this earth. When my friend and I prayed, we asked Jesus to tell our loved ones we loved them and missed them. She told me she was going to start doing that when she prayed.

Don't get me wrong, we shouldn't attempt to contact the dead. Do not place your trust in mediums or channelers. You will waste your time attending a seance. We, nor anyone else, can "cross over" to talk to the dearly departed. The Bible teaches there are no such things as ghosts returning from the grave to roam the earth. When someone dies, they cannot come here and we cannot talk to them. But, if you look at Hebrews 11 and 12 there is an implication that those that have gone on in faith are present in our lives to some extent. Maybe they are present in heaven when we pray. Hebrews 12:1 says, "Therefore, since we are surrounded by such a great cloud of witnesses..." The author is speaking of the list in chapter 11 that had long since departed from this life and are in heaven. Where are we "surrounded?"I believe we are surrounded by them every time we go to God in prayer.

We must not live in a fantasy world, but at the same time we can feel comfort that Jesus knows what we need. There is a great cloud of witnesses who have went before us and are awaiting our arrival. There will be a great reunion one day and the pain of separation will vanish in an instant. Let their faithfulness be our encouragement as we continue our own journey on this earth. I know many people who have found comfort in sensing their departed loved one's presence. It may be a memory stirred by a smell, a sound, or an event. It may be the Holy Spirit comforting us in regard to our loved one. It may be their attendance at our prayer meetings with God. Whatever it is, find comfort in the fact that He is alive and you can trust Him.

Pray: Lord, would You please tell my loved ones I love them and I miss them? Thank You, Lord for our eternal home. Amen.

DAY ELEVEN

GOT STRESS?

Luke 24:19-21 The Message

[Jesus] said, "What has happened?" They said, "The things that happened to Jesus the Nazarene. He was a man of God, a prophet, dynamic in work and word, blessed by both God and all the people. Then our high priests and leaders betrayed him, got him sentenced to death, and crucified him. And we had our hopes up that he was the One, the One about to deliver Israel. And it is now the third day since it happened."

Stress occurs when pressure on the outside overwhelms the pressure on the inside. When external influences disturb the internal equilibrium, and our mind and body begins to be affected. Stress is mostly caused by change. A change in your job, finances, health, physical ability, or prolonged demands on one's endurance will bring on stress. We are amazingly designed by God to withstand a great deal of stress, but for a short period of time. If the nature of the stress is too extreme or intense, the stress-management systems of our bodies will begin to shut down. Constant or reoccurring stress will eventually cause you to become physically ill. Stress will escalate into anxiety, depression, and can cause a person to withdraw from dealing with life.

The two on the road are dealing with their stress with the fight-or-flight response. Since there is no way to fight their way out of this, they are taking a flight. There is a built-in survival mechanism in us that helps protect us from stressful situations. I have felt my body rev up like a racing car's engine before the driver pops the clutch. If there is no way to pop the clutch, the race car's engine will eventually rattle apart if not released. We will eventually rattle apart if left under constant, intense stress. If you remain stressed for a long time, or return to it often enough, you will begin to break down physically and mentally. Stress is one reason they are getting away.

You will never eliminate all stress from your life. Your goal is to learn how to manage or respond to it. A small amount of stress is actually healthy, positive, and will keep you motivated. Our bodies are designed to operate under a reasonable amount of stress. Stress causes us to magnify the situation. When fear enters our faith, we amplify the situation, and use words that are all negative. We also use words like "always" and "never" when speaking of the stressful situation. Everything in their conversation with Jesus is negative. They are speaking of Jesus in the past tense. They mention "it is now the third day since it happened," signifying there was no longer any hope.

Stress can result in burnout. Symptoms of burnout include detachment or withdrawal from people, excessive fatigue, depleted motivation, unexplained exhaustion, apathy, impatience, irritability, inability to concentrate, depression, and obsessive behavior. These are warning signs of stress overload. If you have some of these symptoms, take a look at how Jesus dealt with stress in His life.

- Jesus took regular retreats from the pressures of ministry. He would often put the disciples into a boat and sail to the other side of the sea. He would get alone for solitude and spiritual refreshment and prayer. He prayed a lot and so should we.
- He maintained close, supportive friendships with His disciples, friends like Mary, Martha, and Lazarus. I

believe He laughed and enjoyed life. Laughter is a potent weapon against stress. Laughter triggers chemicals in the brain that fight stress, lift your mood, clear your thinking, and balance your perspective. The Bible says laughter is good medicine.

- Jesus got some exercise. He walked a lot! Exercising thirty minutes a day will bring enormous benefits. Exercise helps you to release tension, helps your circulation, improves your mental alertness, and it just makes you feel better.
- Jesus forgave. He eliminated stress in some situations by releasing those feelings that hold on to bitterness and hurts that had been done to Him. He forgave us.

Stress Is fundamental to life, and is all through the Bible. None of us are immune to stress. All of us can make it through. Jesus wants to help you with your stress. He is alive, trust Him.

Pray: Lord, when I feel stressed please help me to deal with it. Guard my friendships. Apply the good medicine of laughter to my life. Give me the opportunity to get some exercise. Thank You for forgiveness, help me to give it as much as I seek it. Thank You, Lord. Amen.

DAY TWELVE

FINDING FREEDOM IN FAILURE
Luke 24:22-24 The Message

"But now some of our women have completely confused us. Early this morning they were at the tomb and couldn't find his body. They came back with the story that they had seen a vision of angels who said he was alive. Some of our friends went off to the tomb to check and found it empty just as the women said, but they didn't see Jesus."

Who failed? Evidently someone has failed, for you can hear it in their voices. When things do not go the way we planned or expected, we see failure as the result. They are filling their sentences with "buts." The glorious report of their Savior being alive, as reported by them, sounds more like an urban legend. Their explanation of the past few days missed the point. Jesus' death was not the end, but the beginning of their faith and hope.

I have seen so many walk away from God because they felt God was unfair to them. I have visited people who have left the church because they believe something negative happened. I have sat in living rooms listening to families blame their backslidden condition on something negative and now they cannot possibly go back. Jesus is resurrected, they have quit, and Satan has won. Who failed?

Did you ever feel like just giving up? Of course you have, everyone does at one time or another. Has failure ever become your companion? Did you want to quit what you are doing and try something else, somewhere else, with someone else? The two disciples are walking away from Jerusalem and giving up. Their plans and visions for the future went down when the cross went up. They think they have to try something else, with someone else, in Emmaus. One of the hardest things to do when we feel like failure is our companion is to remain where you are and trust in the Lord. We want to be somewhere else. The problem with this plan is that you cannot run from problems. You also cannot hide from God.

Too many try to run away from what they see as failure. Failure can be used by God. He is going to use what they saw as the failure of the cross and the tomb to reveal limitations in their faith. They mentioned they were confused about their women's news. They weren't confused, they didn't believe. They said the women couldn't find Jesus' body. Some of their friends went and couldn't find the body. The two on the road believed Jesus was dead and buried. This was why they were confused, they had limitations in their faith.

God will also use failure to reveal our freedom. There is incredible freedom knowing any problem we have is also God's problem. God's children are God's responsibility. If we are following Him we cannot possibly experience true failure. If we wait with Him we will not fail.

The disciples said the women heard angels proclaiming Jesus is alive. That does not seem to be enough proof for them to accept as truth. We choose freedom or failure. Circumstances do not determine your freedom. Your attitude determines how free you are. Shadrach, Meshach, and Abed-Nego were tied up by King Nebuchadnezzar but were not "free" until they were thrown into the fiery furnace. There, all their bindings were burned off, and they walked with the Son of God (see Daniel 3). In Acts 16 Paul and Silas were beaten and shackled in the deepest, filthiest section of the prison. At midnight they sang and praised God. As a result of their "freedom" the prisoners were freed and the guard's entire family was saved. Circumstances are not your prison bars. The limitations of our faith is what imprisons us. When we limit God in our lives, we lose our freedom to follow Him, and this is true failure. Therefore, what we might see as failure can be an effort to reveal to us God's lordship. It seemed God had failed on Friday according to the two disciples. The darkness of Friday still lingered in their minds and hearts. They had missed the "Sonrise" the women had experienced. They are talking of an empty tomb and their empty hopes. They concluded their explanation with, "but they didn't see Jesus." They were leaving Jerusalem and the empty tomb behind.

We often look for an easier path to walk. Tough times, stress, and even what seems to be total failure are really our allies. We become strong in spirit only as we trust in God. By walking in faith we will experience freedom. He is alive, trust Him.

Pray: Lord, thank You for never failing or giving up on me. Thank You for the freedom of an empty tomb. Help me not to limit you in my life. Thank You, Lord. Amen.

DAY THIRTEEN

KNOWING MORE THAN YOU'RE DOING
Luke 24:25-27 The Message

"Then [Jesus] said to them, "So thick-headed! So slow-hearted! Why can't you simply believe all that the prophets said? Don't you see that these things had to happen, that the Messiah had to suffer and only then enter into his glory?" Then he started at the beginning, with the Books of Moses, and went on through all the Prophets, pointing out everything in the Scriptures that referred to him."

We often forget what God has already told us. We know more than we are doing. I have come to believe my generation is one devoid of theology. Theology means the study of God. This generation is too busy to stop long enough for God to teach them. We are the microwave generation that lives on fast food at a faster pace. God has spoken into the whirlwind of our busy lives without getting a response. You must be still and know that He is God.

In this journey He teaches us. The journey is where the two on the road encounter Him. Jesus begins by calling them thick-headed and slow-hearted. He is calling role to begin class. He asks them, "Why can't you simply believe the Word of God?" When dealing with the Word of God, we must believe that all of it is truth to us or none of it will be. God's Word is our map through life. The Bible will be your way through this, if you will allow yourself to study it. Here are some simple steps to studying your Bible.

- Read the passage. You do not have to read an entire book or chapter, just read what is before you that day. Read until you are touched by the message.

- Reflect on your life. What does the passage say to you today? Where are you in your walk with God? What is He dealing with in your life right now?

- Realize the principle. God wants to talk to you as your Father and your God. He loves you more than you know, and His truths are for you. His principles will speak to every aspect of your life. Listen to what He is saying.

- Respond to the message. If you are unclear, pray for Him to reveal His truth to you. Throughout the day look for opportunities where He will teach you. If His message is clear, respond to Him immediately. Be willing to do whatever His message leads you to do.

- Resolve to take action. Go out and do as you have been taught. Do what you know. Make the decision to live your life today in the will of God. Commit to walk with Him in faith, believing what He has taught you.

God's Word breathes life into us. The power of the Word of God is hard to explain. The Bible provides one of the greatest sources of comfort when you lose a loved one. Jesus came to them in their hour of need and taught them the Word of God. Hebrews 4:12 says, "God means what he says. What he says goes. His powerful Word is sharp as a surgeon's scalpel, cutting through everything, whether doubt or defense, laying us open to listen and obey."

After Brandon's death when everyone else's lives went on as if nothing had happened, I struggled. Why were other's lives going on after my life was so devastated? A dear friend gave me these verses. The power of the living Word of God comforted me.

Isaiah 57:1-2 The Message

[1] Meanwhile, right-living people die and no one gives them a thought. God-fearing people are carted off and no one even notices.

The right-living people are out of their misery, they're finally at rest.

[2] They lived well and with dignity and now they're finally at peace.

And Psalm 116:15 The Message

"When they arrive at the gates of death,
God welcomes those who love him."

The power behind these verses made a big part of my healing possible. God's Word helped give me direction through a painful time. He has a message for you in your journey. He wants you to be able to do what you know is right. He is alive, trust Him.

Pray: Lord, I pray for my generation to have a renewed desire for theology. Allow Your Word to help my healing process. Thank You, Lord for Your powerful, living Word. Amen.

DAY FOURTEEN

WILL YOU LOSE WHAT YOU HAVE
IF YOU GET WHAT YOU WANT?
Luke 24:28 The Message

They came to the edge of the village where they were headed. He acted as if he were going on.

"Because it's there" is the well-known phrase so many use when going after a goal or working toward a desired destination. A thirty-eight year old British schoolmaster named George Leigh Mallory uttered these words in 1924 when asked by a reporter why he was planning to climb Mount Everest. No one else had ever accomplished this task, and Mallory intended to be the first. On June 8th, Mallory left his family, consisting of a young wife and three small children, and began a journey simply, "Because it's there." He never returned. In 1999, seventy-five years later, an American climbing team discovered Mallory's perfectly preserved body on the slopes of Mount Everest. He had not reached the top. A young wife lost her husband and three small children grew up without their father. He sacrificed his life going after an unnecessary goal. He went on a journey to get what he wanted, and he lost everything he had.

Every statement in Scripture is there for a reason. They reached their destination, and the Scripture says Jesus was continuing on. What good is a destination if the end is no better than the beginning? They left Jerusalem thinking they had lost all hope, and went looking for some. We often spend our lives going after the temporary. We move from one temporary destination or goal to another. We say, "Just one more, and I will be happy" or "If I can reach this next level, I will have success." If we reach the next level, we always find it to be another temporary destination. We must stop and ask ourselves, "Will I lose what I have if I get what I want?" Too many times we are ignoring the eternal in pursuit of the temporary. Christ would have continued on without them. When they got to their destination, they found just another temporary success. They needed more.

Those who have lost a loved one live in the suburbs of heaven. It is no longer a place far away in the sky, it is a reality that lives in our hearts and captures our imagination. It becomes our destination in a whole new way. Our journey on this earth is toward heaven. Most of the time heaven seems too far away. It isn't healthy to constantly sit around and daydream about heaven. You will miss what is happening around you. To walk this journey with only the destination in sight can give you tunnel vision. The attraction of heaven is not the streets of gold, the gates of pearl, or a mansion. Heaven is an eternal home. Home is the people you love, not the place you live.

When Brandon died so many people kept telling us not to forget we still had two daughters. I took what they said two ways. Some were saying that we had lost one child but at least we had two others. I dealt with that earlier in this book. A living person can in no way replace a person who has died. The second way I took what they said was that our son was in heaven and cared for. Now you must focus your attention and energy on the ones yet to make it through life. I believe some of their advice was right and wise.

As you continue to recover in your loss, don't miss out on the life that is around you. Your relationships with Jesus and with other loving people in your life has little to do with circumstances. Remember to love them right here, right now. When I am at work my attention must be on the tasks at hand, the deadlines to meet, and the appointments kept. I do look forward to my home, but that must not detach me from my work. When I finally finish for the day and drive up my driveway, I do not look forward to carpeted floors or cushioned recliners. My heart races because there is a beautiful wife and two wonderful daughters inside waiting to greet me. Home and heaven are attractive and anticipated because of its people.

Home is our destination only after we have finished our work. Glance up at your destination often while on this journey. Keep your gaze on your path and your companions. Remember to see the sights, hear the sounds, and smell the aromas. Don't lose what you have in pursuit of what you want. You will get home one day, and you will find loved ones waiting. Especially Jesus. He is alive, trust Him.

Pray: Lord, help me to see the sights, hear the sounds, and smell the aromas of your creation today. Please grant me the wisdom to love the people You have placed in my life. Thank You, Lord for loving me so much. Amen.

DAY FIFTEEN

GETTING INTO POSITION TO PRAY
Luke 24:29 The Message

But they pressed him: "Stay and have supper with us. It's nearly evening; the day is done." So he went in with them.

This verse shows us one aspect of prayer, constraining God. They asked Him to abide with them. They wanted Him to fellowship with them. They asked Jesus to stop and be their guest. They asked God to fellowship with them for a while, and He did. He still does today. He wants you to constrain Him.

The power of prayer has saved cities, healed the sick, raised the dead, closed the mouths of wild beasts, altered the course of nature, and changed lives. God wants us to constrain Him. The hard part is to settle down, and be at home in our prayer closet. We constrain God to stay and fellowship with us only when we settle down and become still. Prayer is the most important thing we will do today. Some days we are fooled into believing we are too busy to pray. We cannot seem to find a time void of interruptions where we can commune with God. Jesus repeatedly went away to a solitary place to pray and commune with the Father. We must do the same.

While sitting with them, He blessed what He was giving them. He gave thanks for what they were about to receive. Jesus broke bread and served them, because they took time to stop and sit with Him. In Luke 10:38-42 is an interesting story. "As they continued their travel, Jesus entered a village. A woman by the name of Martha welcomed him and made him feel quite at home. She had

99

a sister, Mary, who sat before the Master, hanging on every word He said. But Martha was pulled away by all she had to do in the kitchen. Later, she stepped in, interrupting them. "Master, don't you care that my sister has abandoned the kitchen to me? Tell her to lend me a hand." The Master said, "Martha, dear Martha, you're fussing far too much and getting yourself worked up over nothing. One thing only is essential, and Mary has chosen it—it's the main course, and won't be taken from her." Whose side are you on, really? Martha is working and doing everything by herself while Mary's just plain lazy! I mean, after all, Martha is serving the Lord, His disciples, and the rest of her family all by herself. She has worked hard for this visit. She has prepared all the Lord's favorite foods, and set out her best dishes. She has cleaned and dusted for a week. Now when it is time for her to shine as the "hostess with the mostess," everybody ignores her. She is so busy serving the Lord and the others, she cannot enjoy His presence. Her well-intended labor of love turns into anger and accusations, casting a gloom over the entire affair. Her service is distancing her from everyone. Jesus will survive if Martha does not feed Him, but Martha will not survive if Jesus does not feed her. Some are so busy serving, they have no time to sit at His table and feast. Are you taking time to stop and sit with Jesus? Are you willing to stop right now to fellowship with your Lord?

Prayer is surrendering. Surrender is not a popular word for the simple reason it signifies a defeat. When a nation surrenders, the enemy determines the conditions of their defeat. As Americans, we have witnessed the unconditional surrender of other nations to our own. Most of us have sworn in our hearts that we will never be the ones doing the surrendering. Surrender is not a comforting word, unless it has to do with God. Our surrender to God is both dignified and wise.

When we approach God to pray, we must surrender our desires and our will to the heavenly Father like Jesus did. In John 6:38 He states, " I came down from heaven not to follow my own whim but to accomplish the will of the One who sent me." He prayed in the Garden of Gethsemane, "Not My will, but Your will be done." He taught us to pray, "Our Father which art in heaven...Thy kingdom come, Thy will be done on earth as it is in heaven..." When we approach God in prayer we must surrender to His supreme sovereignty. Our lives will go through good times and bad. Our health will decline if we grow old. Some friends and loved ones will hurt us, leave us, and some will die. Some of our fondest dreams will never come true. This is life. In prayer we surrender. We trust God to do what is best. Prayer is the only way to overcome dissatisfaction and anger about uncontrollable circumstances. Go ahead and say, "I surrender all" to the Lord right now. He is alive, trust Him.

Pray: Lord I surrender all to You right now. I desire Your will, not my own today. Thank You, Lord for your sovereignty. Amen.

DAY SIXTEEN

OPENING YOUR TEAR-FILLED EYES
Luke 24:31 The Message
At that moment, open-eyed, wide-eyed, they recognized him. And then he disappeared.

Jesus sat and ate with prostitutes and publicans when He was here. Why? They were willing to be loved. They were reachable because they knew they were sinners in need of help. One reason some have an empty prayer life is because they already know it all before they go. We must go to God expecting to see Him. Go to Him willing to be honest with Him. Our eyes are opened when we approach Him, especially when we arrive with the desire to be loved. We live in desperate times requiring desperate prayers. We must come to the table needy, expecting and willing to be loved. Admit your desperation for His grace. If you do, you will see Him in a new way.

Jesus vanished from their sight when their eyes were opened. They had recognized Him. They suddenly knew He was alive just as He said He would be. He was really alive! Prayer is not our attempt to overcoming God's reluctance. Prayer is not trying to convince Him to bless us. Prayer is going to where He is because you know He is alive.

Since Brandon died I have preached and spoken much about the importance of having an intimate, personal relationship with Jesus Christ. As a result, I have often gone back to the first moment I encountered Jesus, and was "open-eyed" for the first time in my life. I remember how I saw things in a new way. I looked at life with the freshness of being "born again." Jesus was no longer the object of a Bible story. He was not just a name I put at the end of a prayer. He was alive! He loved me, and I loved Him.

When you are traumatized by the death of a loved one, you doubt that such a love could let something like this happen to you. At times Jesus seems so distant. It may seem that He has disappeared. You cry out to Him for answers to your loss and you long for some form of spiritual logic to adequately deal with the pain in your heart.

When you cannot find answers, and He seems far away, remember your first love. Go back to the moment you first met Jesus. Remember that His love for you then is the same love He has for you now. His love hasn't changed. Look back to the same Savior that entered your heart and forgave your sin. Trust anew in His willingness to supply our every need in the perfect way. His love for you is unconditional, and endures anything.

When we go to Brandon's grave, it is often dirty. We have stored brushes under the flower pot on his marker. There is Styrofoam holding the flowers pressed down into the flower pot. When there is a lot of rain, the flower pot fills with water. One day we took out the flowers, removed the flower pot, and got our brushes to clean his marker. As I was pouring the water from the pot onto Brandon's marker, I thought to myself that it looked like a bottle of tears we had shed was being poured on his grave.

That's when God spoke to my heart and told me He kept my tears in His bottle (see Psalm 56:8). He let me know how precious my tears were to Him. This experience helped me to remember His love for me. At that moment I was wide-eyed because I realized my tears weren't in vain.

When you weep over your loss, your pent-up emotions burst through your hurting soul. While tears stream down your cheeks, remember God sees and catches every tear. He opens your eyes after He wipes them. Tears help us to see the source of our hope. In chapter 21 of the book of The Revelation we are told that He will wipe every tear. Our tears matter because we matter to Him.

If He is keeping our tears, there is ever before Him the evidence of our sorrow. He will give you His incredible grace. He will transform your sorrow. He will comfort your fear. He will give you strength and stamina to continue. Jesus will take your tear-filled eyes and open them wide so you can see Him. Remember your first love, especially through the tears. He is alive, trust Him.

Pray: Lord my tears are in Your bottle. I desperately need Your grace to continue. Open my eyes wide so I can see You today. I love You Lord, even through my tears. Amen.

DAY SEVENTEEN

GETTING A WORD FROM GOD
Luke 24:32 The Message

Back and forth they talked. "Didn't we feel on fire as he conversed with us on the road, as he opened up the Scriptures for us?"

When God speaks, things happen. He spoke and the universe was created. God spoke everything into existence. When Jesus spoke, sicknesses disappeared, demons retreated, and the dead were raised. When God speaks to you, things happen in your life. God's voice has a lasting impact on your life.

Our two disciples are experiencing some "holy heartburn." They were experiencing His presence all the way down to their soul, and it felt good. Their hearts were set on fire by the voice of God. Has it been a while since your heart was set aflame by the Word of God?

God's Word is not for entertainment, information, or observation. We become easily bored waiting for God and expect Him to entertain us. We become easily distracted while trying to follow God. We expect Him to tell us immediately about the situation. We observe God at work around us, and decide whether to participate with Him or go do something else. The problem with approaching God's Word this way is that none of these responses require an immediate response from us. When we approach God for entertainment, information, or observation we do not see the need to obey. Their hearts burned within their chests because they took to heart what they heard. His words were not for their entertainment, information, or mere observations. His word was the living and breathing truth about life.

They may have journeyed toward Emmaus to find some answers. They soon realized they didn't get answers from God. Instead they were in the presence of God, who is the answer. When they stopped and began to reflect on what the Scriptures said, and what Jesus revealed to them, it all made sense.

I sat and watched the television screen as the parents of the missing child wept and pleaded for their child's safe return. I was glad I was not like them. I thought something like that could never happen to me or my family. I said a quick, silent prayer for them. I then went on my way believing I was safe from that kind of pain and fear. I honestly never gave much thought to my vulnerability while watching the nightly news and it's reports of the day's tragedies.

As I sat in our kitchen calling the hospital emergency rooms, I was clicking a pen that had Bible verses that turned in the barrel with each click. I was reading the verses still holding to the belief that I was not like those families you see on TV or hear of on the evening news. It seem impossible that death could invade the sanctity of my precious home. My bubble bursted when the State Troopers rang the doorbell. I was told the next day that our story was on the TV news. We have the newspaper article from the local paper in our scrapbook. I had joined the ranks of the bereaved.

I always had true feelings of sadness when terrible things happened to others. I had mentioned how I didn't think I could survive joining the bereaved. How could anyone survive or endure such pain? We survive and we endure by grace. I have learned how grace isn't given until grace is required. You do not have the grace today you will need tomorrow. God supplies grace for you only on the day you will need it.

When tragedy arrives, so does God's grace. God speaks, and His Word becomes our lifeline. When you are living with the belief that tragedy could never enter your family, you know a lot of Scripture that doesn't pertain to you yet. When you join the bereaved, those Words suddenly begin to burn into your heart and your eyes are opened to what they truly mean. God's Word is not for entertainment, information, or observation. God speaks to us to give us hope as our hearts are broken. When God speaks to you, things happen in your life. His Word is relevant and true even when you find your family on the evening news. He is alive, trust Him.

Pray: Lord thank You for my Bible. Help me not to read it for entertainment, information, or with the option to believe it. Thank You for giving me hope as You speak to me. Amen.

DAY EIGHTEEN

IT REALLY HAPPENED
Luke 24:33-36 The Message

They didn't waste a minute. They were up and on their way back to Jerusalem. They found the Eleven and their friends gathered together, talking away: "It's really happened! The Master has been raised up—Simon saw him!" Then the two went over everything that happened on the road and how they recognized him when he broke the bread. While they were saying all this, Jesus appeared to them and said, "Peace be with you."

They got up immediately. Even though it was late, and the darkness was deep, they ran. Why the sudden change in direction? What was different in the journey that caused them to stop doubting and start running? The change occurs when we settle the fact that Jesus is truly alive.

Temptation is the crossroads of the will. We choose to either accept the truth and walk in the light of that truth, or continue the path we are on. They had plenty of excuses to stay. They were weary from the long journey. It was dark, and in the darkness dwells many unseen dangers. They were hungry, and hadn't eaten yet. None of these reasons to stay were enough to hold them. They didn't waste a minute. There was a bigger reason to go. There are tragic results when we refuse to surrender to God. We begin to only go through the motions and call it obedience. There will be prayer, but it will become shallow and empty. There will be praise, but it will be lifeless. There will be participation, but it will be conditional and convenient. The power and the passion will be missing. Going through the motions may be convenient and easy for a while, but it will soon become meaningless. If we continue to go through the motions we will quickly burn out. These two had a burning within their hearts that was not man-made and it drove them out into the night to tell their friends of their experience.

When tragedy has hit your home, you may be tempted to remain in the dark, and just go through the motions. Other people will give you permission to quit. Many may even expect you to. When your walk with Christ is disrupted, you may begin to believe that life will grow increasingly more difficult. Then one day something happens that you don't expect. The darkness you have been walking in parts and some light shines through. Maybe you laugh. Perhaps you look outside at the sunshine and you enjoy it. Suddenly you find yourself surrounded by friends talking away and it really happens. Peace dawns in your soul.

The two disciples returned to Jerusalem a lot quicker than they left it. They joined their friends in the Upper Room. While they were speaking of their experience with the living Christ, He shows up. There is no peace in our souls unless Jesus is in the midst. When He is in our presence, and we acknowledge Him, we will always find peace.

He comes to us. Let that sink in for just a moment. Jesus comes to where we are. Through the darkness, through the locked doors, and in the midst of our disbelief, He comes. Friday's hopelessness is now Sunday's peace. The cross did not stop Him. The grave could not hold Him. Their locked-door-doubt did not keep Him from coming. He came because He wanted to be with them just as He wants to be with you. He comes, bringing peace in the midst of our doubt and our disappointment.

Don't allow yourself to feel guilty for feeling this peace. Breathe in and enjoy these moments God brings you. It is the gift of God, so do not despise it or refuse it. Allow it to really happen. You do not need to explain what has happened to anyone. If someone comments or questions you about how you seem to feel good, don't feel like you must give them an excuse. Don't be ashamed of His peace. Let it really happen. Those who love you will be happy for you. The peace is not because your circumstances have changed, it is because Jesus comes to us. He is alive, trust Him.

Pray: Lord let it happen. Please show me if I begin to only go through the motions and call it obedience. Help me to accept and enjoy Your peace as a gift from You. Thank You, Lord. Amen.

DAY NINETEEN

WALKING WITH A BIG GOD
Luke 24:36

While they were saying all this, Jesus appeared to them and said, "Peace be with you."

I pushed the lawn mower through the thick neglected grass, wondering if I would ever finish the yard before winter. My small son Brandon walked up and put his little hands on the mower handle between mine. If I let go, the grass will not get cut. If I keep pushing, I will have to walk with my legs spread around his little frame. At first I start to tell him to help me later. He could do this when the grass is not waist high, and when I had more time to appreciate his "help." But, he is there to help his daddy cut the high grass. So I hunch my back, spread my legs and do my best not to step on my helper. The cutting continued, but it was a lot slower and more difficult than before. All this because my little son was "helping" his daddy.

Suddenly it hit me. This is how it is when I am "helping" my heavenly Father build His kingdom! I looked down at this little helper and saw my Heavenly Father seeking and saving the lost world. There I was, holding on to the handle. I'm not really pushing, I'm just holding on. I hinder His progress. He could do this work so much easier without me, but He doesn't stop me. He chooses to stoop over and walk with His legs spread around me and let me "help" Him. Why? For my sake. He wants me to have the privilege of doing this with Him. He likes my company. That's why He built heaven, so I could live and walk with Him forever.

Today's verse reveals a really big God. He cannot be stopped even with our help. He is still saving souls and restoring lives and wants us to join Him. What about you, are you holding on and working with Him today? Do you see Him working and motioning for you to join Him? You can, all you have to do is join Him.

People without God have no hope beyond the grave. When they pass through the veil of death they leave behind any hope. Or if they suffer tragedy, they suffer without the presence of Christ. The Resurrection is our hope. We have faith in the God who raised Christ from the grave. We trust in the God who defeated death and promises to raise all those who trust in His Son. This is why we live with hope, we live in the presence of a really big God.

We know how to make it through the tough times of life and this is our peace. In His grace and by His unconditional love we find rest for our weary and hurting souls. Those who trust in Christ have a glorious future awaiting them. We look beyond this life and joyfully anticipate heaven.

We have so much to share with others. So many tragedies happen every day around us and people's lives come apart at the seams. God left us here for a purpose, and it was to join Him in what He is doing in these people's lives. He wants us to share the peace He has given to us. Make the life you have left matter. Give away your hope, share your journey with others.

Since Brandon died I have met so many parents that have lost their children to tragedy. I spoke at a church where two different families came to me at the conclusion and spoke to me how their children had died. One family wanted me to pray with them in the altar and as we prayed together, we shared our pain and also our hope. I have stood with a man who lost his daughter and asked him about his life. He told me how he was surviving each day and we both nodded, understanding some of what the other was feeling.

We walk with a big God, and He is worth sharing with others. Look for opportunities to share what you have. Put your hands to the handle and God will put His hands beside yours and push. Walk with Him and enjoy His presence. Walk with Jesus on this road from Emmaus toward Eternity. He is alive, trust Him.

Pray: Lord You are worth sharing with others. I pray for divine appointments where I can share You with others. Let me put my hands beside Yours and walk with You. Thank You, Lord for Your presence in my life. Amen.

DAY TWENTY

IT'S REALLY HIM
Luke 24:37-47 The Message

"They thought they were seeing a ghost and were scared half to death. He continued with them, "Don't be upset, and don't let all these doubting questions take over. Look at my hands; look at my feet—it's really me. Touch me. Look me over from head to toe. A ghost doesn't have muscle and bone like this." As he said this, he showed them his hands and feet. They still couldn't believe what they were seeing. It was too much; it seemed too good to be true.

He asked, "Do you have any food here?" They gave him a piece of leftover fish they had cooked. He took it and ate it right before their eyes.

Then he said, "Everything I told you while I was with you comes to this: All the things written about me in the Law of Moses, in the Prophets, and in the Psalms have to be fulfilled.

He went on to open their understanding of the Word of God, showing them how to read their Bibles this way. He said, "You can see now how it is written that the Messiah suffers, rises from the dead on the third day, and then a total life-change through the forgiveness of sins is proclaimed in his name to all nations—starting from here, from Jerusalem!"

I awoke one morning and asked the question, "What do I do now?" My days now had a different value. Plans I had made were gone and new plans may or may not come about. I had no "Plan-B" for my life, but now I had to think of one.

114

The entire Bible is filled with disasters and their effects. There have been a global flood, earthquakes, wars, famines, plagues, epidemics, and widespread persecution. In the verses before us we find God's answer to the devastation of life. Jesus says, "Everything I told you while I was with you comes to this." The anticipated answer the prophets sought, the hope of Moses, the questions of life in the Psalms are all answered right here in the appearance of Jesus. Not only the questions of the past but the hope for the future is clearly proclaimed in a locked upper room with a meal of left-over fish and a Bible study. They had seen Him brutally beaten, murdered, and buried on Friday. They mourned deeply Saturday and dealt with the loss of their friend and teacher. They were dealing with incredibly deep emotions, attempting to process everything they were hearing and seeing. Confusion was the main topic of conversation when suddenly He is standing in their midst as they are trying to catch their breath He tells them He is sending them out from there. He wants others to know He is alive and able to help them through.

If you have lost a loved one, you too have ridden the emotional roller coaster of mourning deeply, attempting to process everything, your fears mixed with confusion. In the midst of it all He comes, touches and then teaches you. He will open your understanding of His Word to you. Jesus will begin where you are then He will lead from here. He is sending His people out to proclaim that He is alive to all nations so He wants to start you on your journey where you are.

Survivor Eva Hart remembers that night. It was April 15, 1912, and she was a passenger on the Titanic. She remembers the sound of the iceberg ripping a three hundred foot gash in the starboard side. She still can see the huge ocean liner disappear in only two hours and forty minutes. She recalls, "I saw all the horror of its sinking. I heard, even more dreadful, the cries of drowning people." She was on one of the twenty life-boats and rafts launched. Most of the passengers ended up struggling in the icy seas while those in the boats waited a safe distance away. Lifeboat No. 14 did row back to the scene after the unsinkable ship slipped from sight. Alone, Lifeboat No. 14 chased cries in the darkness. Seeking the icy waters, it saved a precious few. Incredibly, no other boat joined it. Some were already overloaded. Virtually every other boat was half-filled. They rowed aimlessly in the night, listening to the cries of the lost. They feared a crush of survivors would cling to their life-boat and sink it.

God will give you something worth proclaiming. You have met the risen Christ personally in this journey. You may face a large obstacle, the fear of the unknown. People are drowning in dark, cold waters around us. Go to them. Tell them He is alive, trust Him.

Pray: Lord I ask You to use me to help others. I am in this valley with You for a reason. If there are others who need help finding their way to You, send me to them. Lord use me to help others. Amen.

A FINAL NOTE

WHERE DO I GO FROM HERE?
2 Corinthians 4:16-18, 5:1-10 The Message

"So we're not giving up. How could we! Even though on the outside it often looks like things are falling apart on us, on the inside, where God is making new life, not a day goes by without his unfolding grace. These hard times are small potatoes compared to the coming good times, the lavish celebration prepared for us. There's far more here than meets the eye. The things we see now are here today, gone tomorrow. But the things we can't see now will last forever.

For instance, we know that when these bodies of ours are taken down like tents and folded away, they will be replaced by resurrection bodies in heaven—God-made, not handmade—and we'll never have to relocate our "tents" again. Sometimes we can hardly wait to move—and so we cry out in frustration. Compared to what's coming, living conditions around here seem like a stopover in an unfurnished shack, and we're tired of it! We've been given a glimpse of the real thing, our true home, our resurrection bodies! The Spirit of God whets our appetite by giving us a taste of what's ahead. He puts a little of heaven in our hearts so that we'll never settle for less.

That's why we live with such good cheer. You won't see us drooping our heads or dragging our feet! Cramped conditions here don't get us down. They only remind us of the spacious living conditions ahead. It's what we trust in but don't yet see that keeps us going. Do you suppose a few ruts in the road or rocks in the path are going to stop us? When the time comes, we'll be plenty ready to exchange exile for homecoming.

But neither exile nor homecoming is the main thing. Cheerfully pleasing God is the main thing, and that's what we aim to do, regardless of our conditions. Sooner or later we'll all have to face God, regardless of our conditions. We will appear before Christ and take what's coming to us as a result of our actions, either good or bad."

Jesus has promised to return. He WILL take those who believe in Him to live with Him forever in His home, heaven. We are assured that God already knows what will happen. He already has a plan, even in these hard times. We have His promise that He is going to carry us through.

After Brandon died my beard turned white. My wife asked me to color it because she didn't want to be married to an "old man." I told her that I was going to wear a white beard as a symbol of my mourning. After several months, I saw myself in the mirror, and realized how aged I looked since his death. We all grow older, but losing a loved one seems to speed-up the process. I decided to take off my "sackcloth and ashes" and color my beard. I still mourn. I will all of my life, but with hope. I know my son is waiting for me at the end of this journey. You can mourn while refusing to give up. Keep going. Keep walking. Don't give up!

Where do I go from here? I start where I am and go where He leads me. Jesus will lead you through whatever lies ahead in this journey. Then one day the journey will be over for all of us and He will lead us home. He will take us into heaven and introduce us to His Father. He will tell God the Father that we are with Him. Then there will be a celebration. We will have a glorious reunion. We will enjoy our last homecoming.

There will be tears of joy because we will know we will never be separated again. There we will live with Him and our loved ones through eternity.

As the Apostle Paul wrote from a Roman prison, "But neither exile nor homecoming is the main thing. Cheerfully pleasing God is the main thing..." Hold on to the promises while continuing in this journey. Don't sit down and quit, keep going. Do some good with the time you have left. Jesus said in Matthew 16:18, "I will build My church; and the gates of hell shall not prevail against it." Jesus said that His believers would attack the gates of hell. We surely are not attacking those gates to get in! We are to attack the gates of hell to let others out. So many people are prisoners to the lies of hell. Jesus said in John 8:32, "And ye shall know the truth, and the truth shall make you free." We hold our ground and attack the gates of hell with the truth of God. My prayer is that we will stand our ground at the gates of hell. There is a lot of preaching lately that resembles a retreat from the gates. Don't retreat to where it is comfortable or convenient. Stand your ground and see others freed. If you are free, someone remained at the gates of hell with the truth until you came through.

Paul spoke of standing your ground. He said, "Finally, my brethren, be strong in the Lord, and in the power of his might. Put on the whole armour of God, that ye may be able to stand against the wiles of the devil. For we wrestle not against flesh and blood, but against principalities, against powers, against the rulers of the darkness of this world, against spiritual wickedness in high places. Wherefore take unto you the whole armour of God, that ye may be able to withstand in the evil day, and having done all, to stand. Stand therefore, having your loins girt about with truth, and having on the breastplate of righteousness; And your feet shod with the preparation of the gospel of peace; Above all, taking the shield of faith, wherewith ye shall be able to quench all the fiery darts of the wicked. And take the helmet of salvation, and the sword of the Spirit, which is the word of God: Praying always with all prayer and supplication in the Spirit, and watching thereunto with all perseverance and supplication for all saints" (Ephesians 6:10-18 KJV). He encouraged us to remain strong in our stand. Put on this armor every day and attack the gates of hell at every opportunity. You will notice the first article of clothing in this armor is the truth. The truth holds everything else together.

Where do you go from here? You go to the gates of hell with Him. There you stand with Him, and wait for others to be freed by Him. In this journey He has come along side and given you the truth. Get up quickly, run into the night, and set others free. The Apostle John had seen all the glory of heaven. I often cry out his words written in Revelation 22:20-21 (The Message), "He who testifies to all these things says it again: "I'm on my way! I'll be there soon!"

Yes! Come, Master Jesus!

The grace of the Master Jesus be with all of you. Oh, Yes!"

He is alive, and you can trust Him even in the middle of the night.

SUPPORT GROUPS FOR BEREAVED PARENTS

MADD–Mothers Against Drunk Driving
669 Airport Freeway
Hurst, TX 76053
(817) 810-9300

The Compassionate Friends
PO Box 3696
Oakbrook, IL 60521
(877) 969-0010
www.compassionatefriends.org

The Amelia Center
(205) 251-3430
www.ameliacenter.org

SIDS Alliance–Sudden Infant Death Syndrome
10500 Little Patuxent Parkway
Suite 420
Columbia, MD 21044
1-800-221-SIDS

For parents suffering a miscarriage, stillbirth, or other
birth complications:
SHARE
St. Joseph's Health Center
300 First Capital Street
St. Charles, MO 63301
(314) 947-5000

Many local churches and hospitals often sponsor grief
support groups. Some newspapers carry a listing of area
support groups and their meeting times.

SUGGESTED READING

The Bible

Sittser, Jerry. A Grace Disguised. Grand Rapids
Michigan: Zondervan, 1995

Herman, Doug. Faithquake. Grand Rapids Michigan:
Baker Books, 1997

Schiff, Harriet Sarnoff. The Bereaved Parent. New
York: Crown Publishing, 1987

Weirsbe, David W. Gone But Not Lost, Grieving the
Death of a Child. Grand Rapids Michigan: Baker
Book House, 1992

Swindoll, Charles R. Job: A Man of Heroic Endurance.
Nashville Tennessee: The W Publishing Group,
2004

A practical guide for pastors, counselors, and friends:
Wright, H. Norman. Crisis Counseling, What to do and
say during the first 72 hours. Ventura California: Regal
Books, 1993

I will stand beside my son again one day,
because Jesus is alive.